STORMIN' NORMAN B

THE NEW GUV'NOR

STORMIN' NORMAN BUCKLAND

THE NEW GUV'NOR

BY NORMAN BUCKLAND, LEE WORTLEY & ANTHONY THOMAS

AD LIB

First published in 2022 by Ad Lib Publishers Ltd
15 Church Road
London, SW13 9HE

www.adlibpublishers.com

Text © 2022 Norman Buckland,
Lee Wortley and Anthony Thomas

Paperback ISBN 978-1-802470-34-5
eBook ISBN 978-1-786750-71-6

A CIP catalogue record for this book is available from
the British Library.

Every reasonable effort has been made to trace
copyright-holders of material reproduced in this book,
but if any have been inadvertently overlooked the
publishers would be glad to hear from them.

Printed in the UK

10 9 8 7 6 5 4 3 2 1

CONTENTS

FOREWORD – FREDDIE FOREMAN

(THE GODFATHER OF GREAT BRITISH CRIME)

During my many years spent around the great British Underworld I met all kinds of people. From gangsters to pranksters, and minders to movie style romancers, most of whom I left behind. However, when you come across a fella who is moralistically staunch; a fella who doesn't stray from a set of rules he's laid out for himself, from that very first moment you meet them, it becomes instantly apparent that you're in the company of a stand-up fella, and for me, Norman is uncontestably one of the same. Norman is as tough as a bull, yet kind-hearted, but above all he's as honest as the day's long, and extremely good natured. And those ingredients make up for the sort of person I like to have around me.

I first met Norman at a boxing event over in York Hall. He was a little sheepish at first, but I very quickly realised that this change to his customary animated persona was due to the respect he had for the many faces that were in attendance. And in my eyes, something like that speaks volumes about a fella's worth.

Some people are born into the life of street fighting. And with fighting attributes like Norman's, passed down through his Gypsy heritage, I guess it was written in the stars that he would end up using his brawn to feed his family. Much the same as me, people like us are thrown into a certain way of life, and in the same way Mother Teresa flocked to medicine, the likes of Norman and myself heard a different calling. Obviously, you wouldn't say that our career paths ran exactly along the same avenues, but I'm sure that if we had been born into the same era, the two of us would've at one time or another rubbed shoulders with each other, as we pulled in a few quid on some bit of work or another.

I myself was brought up around the Gypsy way of life, with a Gypsy camp right opposite our house and there would be horses and chickens running about all over the place. It was a rough old quarter, but for us as children it was nothing more than one big fairground – it was like a carnival every day. Back then, all of the pubs would be bursting at the seams, and at chucking out time on a Saturday night (due to me being small) I would be lifted up onto a wall so that I, along with my bigger brothers, could watch the big fellas (much like Norman Buckland) on the pavement having toe-to-toe straighteners. So, I suppose in that sense, Norman and I were undoubtedly cut from a similar cloth.

In my senior years, on a couple of occasions Norman has stepped in and helped me out with a few problems. At the time I was in my eighties, and a bit too old to be having punch-ups in the street, and having a fella like Norman in the wings was a great source of support. As well as something that I will always be grateful for.

This book will give you an insight into the life of a street-brawler; a man who fought for a certain echelon's rights at the toughest level. On the other side of the coin, it is a story about a fella who would help anyone out if they were ever in need. It's about a fella who would gift you a nicker if you were ever down on your luck. This book is a testimony to a virtuous man; the inimitable story of a man many thought Britain had long since said goodbye to. I'd also like to mention that I feel it's a book that deserves bestseller status.

All the very best,
Fred

PROLOGUE

Picture a man, he's tall, not excessively so, standing at about five feet eleven in shoes or trainers. However, this man is a spitting and growling street brawler, and when he loses his rag, he grows another six inches and takes on the power and energy of a rhino with the needle. His shoulders stretch out wide to take on the girth of his colossal head and are big enough to fill the widest of nightclub doorways. At first glance, and from a distance, our man looks like your typical streetwalking geezer, but when he moves up close and fills your space, the light from the streetlamps will very quickly become obscured by his frame, and only the faintest glow will be seen sneaking out from the edges.

Imagine the comic book style British Bulldog … yes, you've got it: that big bruiser of a mutt, with a packet of Senior Service ciggies rolled up in the sleeve of its Union Jack vest, and there you have him … that's our man; the obligatory Bulldog of Great British stamp; the prototypical face on every eighties footy fan's rolled-up newspaper cosh. This is the face of fearsome loathing; the screwed up and threatening imagery of everything post-punk Britain hoped to have left behind.

However, he ain't all bad ... oh yes, his bite is *definitely* worse than his fackin' bark. But he can be a loveable and kind-natured geezer, with a quality unfamiliar in a twentieth-century street brawler. He'll help you out if ya need a leg up, and, as Fred says, he'll give you a few bob if you're down on ya' luck. I mean, he's never been one to bite the hand that feeds, but he'll tear ya' fackin' arm off if you give him unwarranted grief.

He's run doors to protect the frightened and has minded the weak, vulnerable and weary. He'll put his life on the line to protect you and will bully the bully who tries to get at you. He has kids in schools who love him, who think he's Santa in a pull-on grizzly bear suit. He's the geezer that everyone runs to, and the one who wrongdoers eventually look up to. He's put many on the right path who were swaying and pulled good out of bad from those who were failing. He's the Godfather of Aylesbury, the loveable lunatic with a key to the town. He's The Guv'nor: he rebukes the heathens and is everyone's friend for all the right reasons.

So, let us introduce you to our man Norman Buckland, or Stormin' Norman as he's known to those who are on familiar terms with him. For thirty-odd years he was known as 'The Guv'nor', and on the streets and in the pubs and clubs, that was how the majority referred to him. And it was true ... well it was at least if that term means a man for the people; a man who would be there 'by your side' through thick and through thin – if that was the case, then he was your man. Back in the 1980s and 1990s he was a respected fist-fighter, with a solid pair of hands to protect you. Stormin' Norman was The Guv'nor: a moniker that was born out of the initial nickname of 'Bruiser', a name that was gifted to him from his late father. His father 'Alfie Snr' who himself was a respected Guv'nor of his manor.

From the Bucklands and the Coopers came a long line of fist-fighters. He had Gypsy Jack on one side, and Grandad Bucky on the other; both of them short in stature yet tasty as fuck in the world of fist-slingers, not to mention both being accepted and rejected in certain walks of life. Gypsy Jack fought the greats on the nineteenth-century unlicensed scene, and his Grandad Bucky fought at the fairgrounds and horse-fairs, for which they were equally accoladed. These men would fight any man, any time, at any destination, and this was the bloodline he sprang from; a character trait he was aware of from the very first day he held his hands up to fight. These tools were a part of him! It was in his bones and in his blood, and there was nothing he could do to rebuff it.

Apparently, after doing a number on one geezer, Norm's great-great-great-grandfather served six months in prison, although, it was said that as soon as he was released from incarceration, he immediately returned to the fight game. And with his new-found notoriety for sending his latest opponent off on a day trip with the undertaker, fear swept through any potential rivals like the plague. Not least, his forthcoming opponent Cabbage, or Stephen Strong, to give his birth moniker. Stephen, or 'Iron-Arm Cabbage' as he was more bafflingly known, was trained by the great Tom Cribb (from Bristol) and Tom Belcher. So, to say he was a well-oiled fighter, is underplaying it a bit.

Norm's Grandad Bucky told him that this Cabbage geezer, 'although older than Gypsy Jack' came out for the fight all guns blazing and began smashing a granny out of him. He said that he'd even dropped his great-great-grandad on his fackin' head, and it was that bad the crowd thought his neck was broken. He also told Alfie that this punishment went on for about twenty-odd rounds. But then, apparently, 'for a second time' he tried picking Jack up and grappling with him, but Jack, being a lot stronger, overpowered him and smashed a devastating shot into his temple which instantly floored him. And that was that ... it was all over, with Norm's great-great-grandad the victor.

It was at this point in the story it became quite clear that Norm's power and will to take a beating had been passed down from Gypsy Jack Cooper. In his heyday Norm was about six feet plus tall and weighed in at around twenty-two stone and Gypsy Jack was just a light middleweight who stood about five feet nine inches in height and was of slight build. Also, we don't know how true it is, but it is believed that to make himself appear taller he stood on his tiptoes. (Mind you, in 1800 and something, at five feet nine inches tall you would've been looked upon as a giant.) But anyway, no matter what size or bulk Norm's great-great-grandad happened to be, he was an awe-inspiring fighter. And, just like Norm, he was equally as dogged.

Anyway, according to Norm's descendants, Gypsy Jack disappeared from London. Legend has it, he was put on a boat and shipped off to Australia marked 'DO NOT RETURN!' However, to be honest, no one really knows the truth, so let's just say it lies deep within the Buckland–Cooper Romany legacy.

Norman began life as a nice boy; a kind-natured little ruffian who just wanted to be loved. And he had no reason to bite – that was until life saw things differently for him and promptly threw a few obstacles in his way. At which point he had no alternative but to fight for what he thought was right. Now, most people would run off and hide! Most people would cower in the hope of becoming momentarily invisible. Not him, he was built from Gypsy blood, and in the silent set of values that were engrained in his brain, the only thing he knew how to do properly was to growl, snarl and hit back at any aggressor. And unfortunately for the wrongdoer, he got fackin' good at it, and on every occasion he hit out with devastating power and ferocity, and it was too late … they were done … beaten, bashed-up and broken, and there was nothing anybody could have done to stop it. Oh, except one thing maybe? They could've left him alone in the first fackin' place, and no one would've got hurt! And for the rest of his existence that's exactly how he would've liked it. But eh, that's not what the big man upstairs had planned for him, which is something you will very quickly find out as you flick through the pages of his life.

INTRODUCTION

It takes a different kind of man to muster up the will to fight and having ancestry like Gypsy Jack Cooper (with all his fist-fighting mastery) urging you on invisibly from beyond the stars, certainly makes the fear in you subside, which in turn diminishes the terror witnessed from behind the boxer's wall of ropes. And for our protagonist Stormin' Norman, no truer affirmation could be noted. For Norman 'The Guv'nor' Buckland held his trophies as rewards of a better life, over that of jewels of arrogance to bolster his accelerating reputation.

So, the buck stopped in Buckinghamshire. For this was the county where reputed yet loveable fist-fighter and hopeful light heavyweight boxer Norman Buckland's forebears chose to plant their family coat of arms. A market town that would one day witness the dawning of Stormin' Norman Buckland, as he, with his overwhelming yet enigmatic demeanour, graced the streets like a prowling lion, duty-bound to seek out unruly outlaws with the hope of setting them on the straight 'n' narrow, affording them a more gratifying pathway to tread.

You see, during the time of his youth, Stormin' Norman, or 'The Guv'nor' as he is respectfully known, was himself something of a disorderly life-force, and instead of opting for a twenty-foot sheet of governed canvas, he chose the avenues and alleyways to utilise his craft. Because at this time in his life, an adrenaline-fuelled Norman saw accolade in the words spoken among 'the chaps', over that of testimonies set by the hierarchy at the British Boxing Board of Control.

Born from fine Gypsy stock of considerable renown, Stormin' Norman fought for honour against the toughest in the land and brought fresh hope, and a sense of dignity to a 'Guv'nor sized' mitt full of failing adolescents who had fallen by the wayside and wound up at Her Majesty's Pleasure. A place that would, as a rule, present them with adequate tools to further their criminal dexterity. But not with The Guv'nor at the head of the class, because, with our man at the helm, the mantra would be for positive progression and a more plentiful life. The case in point being one young man Norman took under his belt: Matt Legg, a wayward boy with no sense of direction, who in the rise of the nineties was heading directly for despondency and degradation, only to be schooled by our protagonist, and who would one day don a pair of eighteens, to fight the fight of his life against Olympic champion and soon-to-be British Heavyweight Champion of the World, Anthony Joshua.

In the eye of the storm of the late raving 1980s, Norman and his brothers, 'chosen by fate', fought toe-to-toe against the country's finest, and like gladiators of the modern-day, though battered, bruised and fading, always came home to tell the stories of how they prevailed.

During his time spent in a thousand rough-house brawls, Stormin' Norman very quickly discovered that his bark was equally as effective and intimidating as his bite, and this hands-off device would often stop in its tracks the nastiest of bar-room brawls. Pull a knife on The Guv'nor, and he will instantly dispatch you and your tool and send you back to school. And in a ploy to put out a fire before the flames licked higher, Norman would ease you out with his overbearing and kindly manner, putting you back in your box without a fist being flung.

In later years, as he approached half a century, Norman took to the ring for prize-fighting fame and beat every man-jack of 'em that were foolish enough to step-up into his space. And with added captivating notoriety, Stormin' Norman's ringside escapades, echoed up and down our green and pleasant land, and a tsunami of documented anecdotes, became the talk among many bar-room males, as Stormin' Norman's vocalised declaration, 'Who's The Guv'nor?' very quickly set sail.

Today, in his fifties, Stormin' Norman, with knife wounds and a shrapnel-filled chest as badges of honour, has decided to settle down. Accompanied by his soulmate and sister-in-arms to guide him, Norman has chosen to cast aside his 'fists-for-hire' CV in favour of a more harmonious and comforting existence for him to settle into. A polar opposite way of life to that of the one of prominence and allure that he once led. And as you read Norman's story, you will very quickly realise that this terrifying growling teddy bear could be one-third of all of those parts, but the fact of the matter is this: the decision would be yours, as to which one of those parts you chose to unleash.

As part of the narrative and to set certain records straight, the text below describes how we see Norman's place in the world of unlicensed, and bare-knuckle fist-fighting!

In and among the 'unaffiliated' fighters of the twentieth and twenty-first centuries there have been many prize fighting Guv'nors; Roy Shaw and Lenny McLean being two of the most recognised and featured in broadcasts. Roy, with a sawn-off and a prayer, went to work with a Robin Hood mentality, as he pinched from those in clover to line the pockets of a lawless community. Not to mention his prison capers that almost brought on his lunacy, requested, and liquid-cosh injected, by the white-coats at a well-known infirmary for the criminally insane.

Next came McLean, with his self-stated, albeit disturbing, prerequisite for violence. Now, this man was of a different time altogether. McLean walked the streets of East End London like a star from film noir; an oversized Rocky Sullivan (from the old film *Angels with Dirty Faces*, starring James Cagney) but with malevolence coursing through his veins. In contrast to Roy Shaw, Lenny McLean only teetered on the cusp of the criminal underworld, as he worked as a money-getter for the gangsters of the time; an enforcer for the retrieval of monies owed that had 'supposedly' fallen by the wayside.

Which brings us to our third successive, although not final, Guv'nor, Stormin' Norman Buckland. Now, this Guv'nor (who currently holds the Roy Shaw EBF Guv'nor belt) is a mix of the two, but with Santa Claus thrown in to balance out the scary side. This Guv'nor fought a similar fight to Roy and Len but for a whole host of different reasons. You see, Stormin' Norman never once courted violence, but, like a challenge to a gladiator, the gauntlet was simply thrown down in front of him, and on most occasions Stormin' Norman and his brother had no choice but to fight for their lives and for the honour of their family name: a name that is inked for all to see in the historical transcripts of the Romany.

From an early age, and partly due to circumstances, these two mighty Buckland brothers were thrust into a way of life with a totally different ethos, and from that day to this, Stormin' Norman and his brother Alfie, felt propelled to hone in on their God-given talents and help the needy, while inadvertently guiding the socially inept and unruly. And as the years fell away, the family name Buckland became equally as ubiquitous as that of their champion fist-fighting great-great-grandfather: Gypsy Jack Cooper.

Now if that ain't a verbal straightener that stakes a claim to what Norman has earned, I really don't know what is. Anyway, all of the above is in the past for him now, so let's get on with what's important … His story.

1

THE BUCK STOPPED IN

BUCKINGHAMSHIRE

Writers' Note:
These days, the youth seem to favour weapons over fists: youngsters don't seem to know any other way. It's crazy what the young'uns will do for a bit of easy money, they don't want to graft for it; they seem entitled and think that a reputation will be handed to them on a plate; they seem to think that a quick cowardly stabbing will be accolade enough to gift them a step-up to the villains' premier league. In our protagonist's day, things were a bit more gentlemanly, and a belt on the chin was usually all it took to put to bed a bit of grief. No one had to get carved-up, no one had to be killed, problems were settled on the cobbles, and spoken about in hushed bars and spielers governed by the Godfathers of the criminal hierarchy.

Fighting for a living ... who wants it? Well, I fackin' didn't. I suppose destiny just had it in for me. Yeah, that's it, all the wrongdoings at the hands of my forefathers were laid at my door, and I got the blame for what had gone before. I can't say I totally believe all of that pony, but eh, if it helps me sleep. Still, anyway, for as far back as I can remember, I've had to fight with my fists to get a move up the ladder of life. But listen, just 'cos I've fought all my life doesn't mean I'm a

23

bully-boy; I've never been a bully, I fackin' hate bullies, you can ask any fucker that knows me. I detest 'em! They suck the life right out of people and it's a horrible way to be.

Look, some people are born to go toe-to-toe. Some people don't scare as easy as others, and I'm a man born out of that breed, I can take punishment and I can give it … tenfold. And my upbringing that you'll read about as the pages flick by, will hopefully make you see things from my point of view.

'Ere, what's that old saying? 'It's not the size of the dog in the fight, it's the size of the fight in the dog?' Well, something like that? And yeah, I'd say that's true. Still, for me it's more to do with his will to survive that keeps him alive, and the same could be said about me. I mean yeah, okay, so I'm a big lump who looks like a fackin' bulldog. But I didn't always look like that: I didn't always look like a bulldog, and if you don't believe me, have a butcher's (butcher's hook − look) at the centrefold pictures. I was a little blond, angelic-looking geezer. 'Ere rein it in Guv, ya' starting to sound aggressive! But I ain't, it's just me, it's just my way and I've always been the same: boisterous, bolshie and like a bull in a china shop. I don't mean no harm, and I never meant to do anyone any harm. But people just have to fackin' push me! Sometimes people don't even listen when you growl at 'em, and that right there unleashes some unholy 'beast' in me! Well, that's what I call it anyway. I've always called it 'The Beast', 'cos that's how it feels; that's how it acts. Because on occasion, this thing rears its ugly head, and I can't do a thing about it. Lee 'my writer' says it envelops me. Fuck knows what that means, what, it covers me in paper that you lick-n-stick and send off to some chosen destination? Well, I don't know about all that, but all I'll say is it takes me over, and I just have to try and control it.

To be honest, I'm a real gentle-natured kind of bloke. But when you did the job I did; when you had to go to work on the door and that, you had to turn it on, you had to flick that switch and animate your character a bit. And, what I found over the years was that this character I'd awoken from deep within me: this loud booming lunatic gorilla, was a frightening beast to the pub- and club-goers. This gorilla simply had to holler at them in a loud, unwavering, scary way and they'd shit themselves and do as they were fackin' told. And it worked! You see, a lot of these venues I'd work by myself, and these groups of fellas could be stood ten handed, and at times they'd need a bit of a hefty shove. Perhaps their fathers should've adopted the same ideology indoors, and then these boys might've done as they were told when they were out entertaining their pals. Even as late as last year, 2019, I'd be stood at that lonely door by myself. Mind you, sometimes the governor of the gaff would say, 'Norm, why don't you bring your wife along for the evening?' and there she'd be, sat outside watching over me. I know it seems crazy doesn't it, having your little petite Missus watching your back. Thing is, the governor probably knew I'd be'ave myself if 'her indoors' was parked up watching over me.

In later years, with my Nanette by my side, I've learned to tame it a bit – I've left the beast in its box, hidden away until the next time it's required to make an unwelcome appearance. But back in the day ... fackin' hell, back in the 1980s and 1990s the beast was there most of the time, looming over me like a shadow, aiding 'n' abetting my violent outbursts and stoking them to their peak. Mind you, in those days some of the lunatics deserved it: some of those nut jobs would've killed me if I hadn't put them away with a swift right-hander. Mind you I was always nice to 'em: if they were bits of kids, I'd pay for a taxi and send them home to their mum.

In my opinion, on the streets, when you're minding some geezer, you have to let your reputation do the talking, and most of the time it works. But every now and then you get the odd lunatic who's every-inch the lunatic you are, and with a special kind of scowling and growling, you have to convince him that you'll go that extra yard … convince him that you're prepared to kill him if he doesn't put you away quick and fast.

Now, in the clubs and pubs it can be a little different, and in my job as a bouncer I learnt very early on to let my persona do the talking, and on most occasions that same scowling growl I just mentioned got the job done. I've had many groups of fellas quaking in their Nikes as I've gently sidled up behind them and shouted, 'Come on, drink up your fackin' booze, I wanna get home and get back in me cage!' And with the fear I'd just put in them, most of them would spill the last few drops of their Grolsch all down the front of their hundred note (£100) Pringle jumpers. Hundred fackin' notes for a bit of wool with a blue lion stamped on it? I know, it's crazy isn't it, but back then, they'd rob the local vicar for a Tacchini tracky top and a pair of kickers.

But I'll get to all that later. Let's go back to when I was a boy.

Growing up we literally had fuck all! I mean it! I honestly thought we were tramps. All the other kids down our street had new bikes, new clothes, the fackin' lot. But me, I thought I was posh if I changed my undies (underpants) more than once in a year. But it didn't matter to me, I didn't get down about it, I just thought I was a bit different – which I was.

I remember when my nutty mate (no names though, 'cos he's in a high-powered job these days) used to pinch clothes off his neighbours' washing lines, and when I was round his house, and I walked past his bedroom, I'd spot all these smart fackin' clothes and think to myself, oh nice one, a sea cadet jumper … now that's a bit o' me … I'll have that! Anyway, I'd wear them down the street and when the neighbours spotted me in them, they would chase me up the road to get them back. Mind you, I was a bit soppy, I'd never learn, 'cos I'd wear 'em again if my mate got hold of any more. But like I said, I was a bit of a tramp, so any bit of clobber that was half decent was as rare as rocking-horse shit to me.

Alfie was a lot sharper in the brain than I was; Alfie says he has himself down as the George Milton to my Lennie Small from a book by a geezer named John Steinbeck called *Of Mice and Men*. I mean, I wasn't thick, I was just illiterate, so at times I imagine it made me feel a bit lost. Alfie used to say that with my love for animals I was like the real-life Lennie. He said I was that big and powerful I'd probably hurt them by over-cuddling them, which given the evidence was probably true, but I've never hurt an animal while nurturing them – that would kill me! I know how to handle them gentle you see, 'cos I've always had a knack for knowing when and where to use my power.

My dad knew how powerful I was, and he knew how well I could take a beating. When I was a young boy, he'd give me a right belting and I would just take it. I wouldn't whimper at all and Dad would say, "'Ere son, you're a little twat you are … you just don't seem to feel it! I'm gonna stop hitting you because it's doing you no good at all … you never seem to learn, boy!' And he was right, and that's how I've been my whole life. But he was wrong about one part, 'cos it did do me some good; it taught me how to take punishment. In the past, many of my opponents have been far better boxers than me, but they just couldn't take the beating like I could. And after a toe-to-toe, be that gloved up or bare fist, that would be the reason they would lose; it wasn't 'cos I was a better boxer than them, it was simply down to the fact that I had a harder shell – I was just a tougher nut to crack.

When we were at infant school, me and my pal Gus used to play with the cars and soldiers and that, and because he always had that thieving mentality 'like one of Fagin's gang', he'd nick them and because of who I was, because of my family background etc., I would get the blame for it, and that little bastard Gus would get off scot-free.

I remember him doing it one time and I got an almighty beating with a sand-shoe. Gus and Alfie were always getting me in bother. But I didn't dislike anyone for it, I didn't blame anyone, I think it was because back then life was cruel, so getting accused of something and getting a beating was just part of life, but even then, I knew not to grass anyone up.

And in later years when I boxed, I used to like taking a beating: I used to like taking someone on who could have a right ol' tear-up. It was crazy too, because even as best pals Gus and me used to be scrapping with each other all the time. I remember one time when we were only kids, and I was smashing into Gus, and he just wouldn't let up. Then, a bit later on in the day he sauntered up, cheeky like, and pushed me clean off a wall, fackin' winded me it did, and with that he's jumped on me and was smashing punches into me. Anyway, I thought, he ain't getting away with that, so next day I called round his house to see if he was coming out; all day I was knocking but Gus wasn't having any of it … he wasn't stupid … he knew I was gonna give him a beating.

Years later I'd go around Gus's now and again and his mother would make me food, we had fuck all, it was hard times although we did well now and again because my brother was a clever sod and he used to get us food.

We used to go shooting, rabbits and all fackin' sorts, but Alfie would turn the gun on us boys and fill us full of lead. I think he thought he was John Wayne or something – he was a rotten bastard, but in a good way. It was all just a bit of fun, and like I keep saying, it's just how it was in those days.

You see, back in the 1960s stuff like that was just stuff boys did for a bit of entertainment, but today you'd get in big trouble; these days they'd probably say it was ABH (Actual Bodily Harm) or attempted murder and they'd haul you up in front of the beak (magistrate). Perhaps on a good day you would end up in therapy – the world's gone mad.

One day Alfie pulled out this big rifle, looked down the sights and said, 'Right ... you've got twenty seconds and then I'm going to start shooting!' With that all the boys began running for their lives. But not me, I was a lunatic, I just ran at him, laughing while he fired loads of lead into my chest. The boys would always call me a fackin' lunatic but it was just the way I was brought up, I didn't have a care in the world.

Mind you, who would have known that years later the doctors at the hospital would ask me if I'd been shot in the chest because they found shrapnel pieces embedded under my skin; no wonder I had problems with my heart from an early age. But eh, that was Alfie, he was just a bit wild like that. Not anymore though, ooh no! We ain't allowed to talk about the old days now that he's a mason or something, 'cos I think they'd kick up a right fuss if they knew about the antics he got up to in his youth.

I remember one time me and him were gonna have a fight and he ordered me down to the local orchard. Anyway, when we got there, he crept up, quiet like, and smashed a bit of wood over me bonce (head). 'I'll 'ave you for that Alfie James Buckland!' I shouted. 'I'll fackin' 'ave you!' And I did, many times. Alfie was a bit of a rebel back then, but like I said earlier, he probably wouldn't admit to it now.

'Ere, talk about being a rebel without a cause (as in the famous old James Dean film), well this dog we had called Rebel was more like 'Rebel without a clue'. Our dad brought Rebel home one day, it was given to us from our Uncle Danny. It was a Dobermann, and when my pals used to come round to the house to call for us the dog would attack them – it was fackin' mental. It must've had rabies or something! Honest, the crazy fucker should've been put down the day it was born! It was a raving lunatic and probably bit the other puppies the minute its mother gave birth to it.

Due to the door work Dad did he would always be working late, which meant that me and Alfie would be home alone a lot. Anyway, that lunatic dog would chase us around the house growling and barking and going off its nut. We ran up and down those stairs like fackin' yo-yos trying to get out of its way.

We'd have scars everywhere from it attacking us. Recently, I said to Uncle Danny while laughing, 'That thing had bitten everyone in the pub and the landlord didn't want it, it was fackin' vicious and should have been put down, but instead you thought you'd give it to us.' Danny laughed and said, 'Yeah, but I knew you would eventually settle him down, Norm.'

One night I was in my bedroom playing with Gus and my mate Jenkins. It was wintertime and the nights were dark very early. Next thing ya know Alfie flung open the door and he had Rebel with him who looked like he was ready to kill as he was snarling at us. Suddenly, Alfie threw Rebel in the room, switched off the light and me and Gus started fighting with each other to get to the window, while all the time the dog was trying to kill us – in the end we managed to clamber out of the window. My brother used to get the hump if we went away, so he'd jump out of somewhere with boxing gloves on and make us spar with him.

Saturday morning consisted of going to the pictures. Films that stick in my mind were *Flash Gordon*, *The Three Stooges* and *The Lady and the Tramp*. We would pop to the chip shop next door for a quick snack beforehand and after we'd go to the underground market pissing around on the escalators – great memories.

As far as education was concerned, I was never very successful … no good at class! You see, in my world, sat with a bunch of kids who moved on quicker than me was always a little off-putting. But just around the corner was a lifeline, because while using the inside of a torn-off cereal box, my gran would teach me about the letters of the alphabet and how you could form them into words. I could take to this concept; it was easier for my brain to take it in. Plus, the fact that the inside of the cereal box was a kind of brown instead of the brilliant white of exercise books helped, which will all be explained later. Mind you, I imagine the reason I could take it in better was mostly due to the hands-on, one-on-one attention my gran provided.

Who would have thought that many years later, in prison of all places, I'd be told that I was actually suffering with a condition called 'Topic Sensitivity'. It was a colour-blind problem that made the letters and words jump around on the paper – which explains everything. This was a life-changing moment for me because it made me feel better about myself;

I no longer felt useless with the tag of somebody who was illiterate, which was something that many simply saw as an excuse for me to be lazy during my years in early education. I knew in that moment that I was actually different from most people and that's why they treated me like the village idiot.

As a boy I remember going to boxing shows. We were born out of the Hardy family, and the Hardys had a big fackin' rep (reputation) as fighting people and were very well-known around the manor (area). At that point in my life, I had no idea that fighting was to be my future, but with the obvious lack of grass-roots education what other path was laid out for me?

You see it's strange for me 'cos deep down I love people; I love helping people and looking out for them. But it was a harsh existence and I had to learn the hard fackin' way, and as I struggled my way through life, I instantly found out how cruel life was, and for that matter how cruel certain individuals could be. And this was the reason why over time this unearthed a beast in me; a beast that showed no mercy; a beast that I had to fight with on a daily basis and keep on a very short leash.

At times it was like taming a rabid fackin' Rottweiler! But this one was worse, 'cos this beast was inside of me, and hitting myself over the head with a piece of four-by-two timber just wasn't an option. Having said that, I was wild at the time and probably wouldn't have felt it anyway. Which is the reason why I won all of my fights. You see, on the pavement I've never been beat! Because, as I keep saying, I could take all the punishment people dished out to me, and then, when they'd run out of juice and their engine had stalled, the beast would come out to play, and most times, the results of my actions would be devastating.

Not for me, but for the poor cunt I was unleashing it on. As a young child, and because my life experience was so cruel, I promised myself that I'd never be bullied and that I would give everyone the time of day if they treated me properly. There are some bad people out there, and you just have to try your best to stay away from them.

When I was about seven Mum and Dad went through a bit of a messy divorce and me and my brother Alfie were packed off to Valencia to live with our gran. Now most people would think, what are you griping about? That sounds fantastic! And it was, but a broken home is a broken home, and deep inside the reality of that probably affected me without me even realising it.

You see, I've bobbed-and-weaved my way through life from the very first moment I could crawl. Battling the elements and everything that came with it − be that celluloid or living, it's just the way I am. There ain't many people like me, who just carry on in full-on attack mode. Most people simply lay down and take it, but not me … not this fackin' geezer. I'm a born fighter, and I'll fight it until the day I shuffle off this mortal coil − it's just the way I am. I've always been the same. I'm an immovable force: loud, impacting, and ready for anything. So, dealing with a move to sunnier climes was a walk in the park for this young whippersnapper.

2

ENGLAND 2 – SPAIN 0

Writers' Note:
As a young boy growing up in the 1960s, life on your own manor could be taxing enough; living among like-minded boys brought up with similar backgrounds could be seen as some death-defying and alarming battleground. But for two oddly spoken boys living what seemed like a million miles away, in a place they'd only heard about on the news, now this, albeit unintentionally, could pull up an avalanche of negative surprises.

The sun was beating down, which made a refreshing change from the cold and dismal days back in good ol' Blighty – and rolling around having a tear-up with your brother in the hot Spanish sun is a whole new ball game compared to scrapping in the mud on a dismal and boring British Monday morning in May. Oh, and that bright, almost crimson, burning Spanish sun I'd heard a lot about, really was different to the insipid orange fucker we were used to back home. I'm only joking … course I'm fackin' joking! Listen, fighting is fighting, and to be honest I couldn't give two flying fucks if that means having a tear-up in a rubble-filled scrapyard or having one on the hot golden sands of Jávea (Xàbia) near Alicante.

Because, my friends, where I come from, a row is a row, and the complimentary imagery and scene setting doesn't play a single part in it. I mean, I'm The Guv'nor, and this Guv'nor will wade in and have a go on any day, in any way, and as long as I do the necessary, I don't care where I am. But as is always the way with me, when the job's done, I'll politely tip you a wink, and while 'Who's the Fackin' Guv'nor?' is playing in loops around my head, I'll say, 'Sorry me ol' mate … but you've just had a visit from Stormin' Norman.'

The year was 1971, and there we were in the sunny climes of Valencia in south-eastern Spain, but to those of you like me, who were too busy 'bird watching' out the windows in school, it's a forty-minute bus ride from Benidorm – 'Ere, now I got your attention, haven't I? Anyway, we were the new kids on the block, and easy fackin' pickings for the local nutters who were out to prove a point. Look, I'm aware that our mighty footballing lions don't do too well battling with these boys in the World Cup on a footie pitch, but challenge me and my brother to an all-in brawl and it's the Spanish boys who are quickly going to get relegated.

But before we get to the Brits going into battle, I wanna tell you a bit about our gran…

My grandmother was strict, that's the way it was in those days. She had lived through the First and Second World Wars and had seen some frightening stuff. I remember her telling us that the dogs in their area must've had a premonition, 'cos they used to howl at the sky before the German planes came over, while Gran and her siblings would run down to the Underground train stations to hide. She said that when they finally dared to venture out after the bombing it would be a right disaster and there would be body-parts of the locals all over the place; I couldn't even begin to imagine what they had gone through. I used to think, no wonder they became tough and not scared of anything.

Gran was a proper little firecracker. So that must be where I get my 'don't give a fuck' attitude from. If we got in a fight with some of the locals and Gran happened to be close enough to see it, she'd quickly run in and start beating on them herself. I'm telling you – she was as nutty as a … Oh shit, I can't think of something with loadsa nuts in it, can I? Anyway, you know where I'm coming from. Right, where was I? Oh yeah. So, if these kids' fathers came out shouting and fackin' hollering, our Gran would steam into them as well; like I said, she didn't give two-fucks for nobody. I mean, our gran's great-grandad was a champion fighter, so his fist-fighting weaponry had obviously sifted its way down through the DNA and landed smack-bang right there in her fiery little frame. And oh, was she fiery: she used to beat the shit out of us with a snake-headed wooden walking stick – I imagine she had problems in her head too, 'cos she used to laugh while she was hitting us with it; it wasn't altogether fackin' human! She would beat me and Alfie black-and-blue, this made me wild … like a caged animal! Mentally, I couldn't deal with it so I'd make my peace physically by fighting, and that way I could release any demons that were rooted inside me. I swear to God I would never treat anyone the way I was treated, I really didn't know what was coming next – I thought I was broken, useless. I honestly didn't think I had a future.

From an early age I knew I had to keep a tight grip on the reins and take control of what was burning inside me. I used to take that much pain, so much so that when I got older and grew big, people could kick ten tons of shit out of me – ten-handed gangs would attack me, but they just couldn't hurt me the way I was hurt as a child. And when their onslaught ceased, I'd get angry, unleash the demons and hit back. It was obvious to me that one day I would be pushed to the point of no return – it was coming! Because, like I've said, as a young boy I was tortured so badly and cruelly, you could beat on me forever and I wouldn't feel a fackin' thing.

It's not nice to admit this, but back in the day my gran would embarrass me in front of the locals, telling them that I was illiterate; as if I was some sort of fackin' idiot, and all because I struggled with the reading and writing and that. I felt useless, it knocked all the bollocks out of me; I was like a dead animal, and due to this downtrodden feeling the will to fight grew stronger in me. I'm sure you can all imagine how that affects you as a boy, knowing that your gran thought those things of you … I s'pose to the outsider, and people who didn't know me, I was like a caged fackin' animal, the pain of all of this was ruining me inside. But I never let on: I just kept on fighting, moving forward. For my sanity alone I just knew I had to keep on keeping on.

I didn't feel like a human being, I'd been turned into an animal at a very early age, physically and mentally abused like a dead animal. I'm going to leave this here now, because I get very, very angry! I haven't felt this anger for such a long time, so I need to settle down and relax before it takes a hold of me.

Honestly, I thought I'd end up a nobody; a gofer (someone who fetches and carries for his boss); an empty vacuum with no accolades to speak of and, if I'm honest, that prospect still haunts me to this day. I imagine that's why I have always felt like this beast inside of me. I never used to be able to keep it under control, but today I do, I have lovely people around me who make me feel worthy, not least of which is my beautiful wife Nanette. She's my safe haven, my sanctuary, and without Nanette I probably would be that empty vessel still searching for some kind of tranquillity. Goodness knows what I'd be getting up to if I had never had her by my side, guiding me. And like that song from that band, the something Roses I think they call 'em, anyway their song goes: 'I'd rather be no one than someone with no one!' And it's true I tell ya, 'cos what's the point of being a 'somebody' who no one even likes? I'd rather have piss-all to my name and still have respect.

Gran also possessed some very clever mystical magic, that must've been passed down from the Romany, she used to read our tea leaves and tell us all kinds of crazy things that were about to happen to us – and believe me she wasn't bullshitting. I remember one time she told us that one day on our way to school we would hit a bridge and there would be an accident.

Anyway, this one particular day, as Alfie and I were hitchhiking to school we got a lift from this geezer – I think he was a Dutchman. Anyway, as he got round this bend in the road suddenly his car was thrown right over and into some bushes; we all managed to escape, and the Dutch geezer said that it must have been the wind that blew the car and made it fly into the bushes the way it did. The only thing was, there was no fackin' wind to speak of, the air that day was as calm as anything. But yeah, it was mental how Gran could see things.

She also said that at school one day we would end up underneath a big crowd of kids and would possibly get hurt from the impact. And, true to her words, one playtime me and Alfie ran out of the class with the rest of the class running behind us, and suddenly … BANG … we tripped each other over and landed in a great big heap on the pissing floor, with the rest of the kids landing right on top of us, it was a nightmare. Our grandmother was a very spooky lady, she would predict things all the time and they would come true. Unfortunately, none of her predictions were ever positive, she never predicted the numbers for the Lottery or which horse was gonna win the National that year. No, most of her predictions were of bad news, and sometimes even bleeding frightening stuff.

The strange thing was, we were only supposed to go to Spain for two weeks, well, that's what we got told at the time, so really, we were dumped there. Well, at times it felt like we'd been palmed-off, 'cos at that time, for the life of me I just couldn't understand why my mum was so upset and crying all the time, and I remember thinking this is going to be the longest two weeks in my life! Who'd have thought that it was actually going to span over the next five years? Me and Alfie were only kids and had no choice in the matter; we just had to get on with it. Our Alfie went home after a couple of years, but I had to stay on.

I love the Spanish people and I still have Spanish friends over there but to really get on I needed to speak Spanish and, as you know, I had no education. I went through life without any education, which was my mistake. I just had to learn the hard way. I did try to learn but was completely useless and I was clumsy as well. Everything I touched got bust-up and broke! At this point in my life I felt like a boy without a future, but I knew that if I wanted to be somebody, I'd have to at least learn to do something, or I might as well be dead.

I knew I was in trouble right from the very start; I knew I was different to everyone else, and that I was an embarrassment … a let-down; I was nothing more than the village idiot. But I'd had enough, something had to give. However, I didn't make it by being educated, in fact that was a dead-end street, but I reckoned that there had to be another way I could get on in life.

You see, when I get tired or angry my words come out all boss-eyed, and that makes me even more angry.

At times I'd sit and think that there was no future for an idiot like me. It was hard, because I love everyone, but 'cos my kindness was mistaken for weakness it seemed to make me a target. So I swore to myself back then that I would never ever treat anyone the way I was treated, and that right there is something I've always stuck to. People can be so cruel, which was something I quickly found out. And with no parents to guide me, look after me or protect me, this boy had to harden up … and quick! It was either that or be pissed on for the rest of my fackin' life.

There's always a bully; always some little arse'ole who wants everyone to think he's the toughest in the land, and it was no different over in Spain; the same bully-boys speaking a different fackin' language, and we fought with them on a daily basis. Having said that, they weren't all like that, no, most of the boys over in Alicante were nicer than your own. But yeah, there were plenty of others who wanted to have a row with a couple of new boys from Blighty and we wasted no time with 'em.

We fought them all the time and won, and they very quickly realised not to fuck with the Buckland brothers. Listen, I don't mean that in an arrogant way; I don't mean to sound like we were the Kray Twins or something, but, the way they stood shoulder to shoulder and took on all-comers was the same way that me and Alfie did – so in that way we were similar. But in no other way though, 'cos at times those two were a couple of fackin' bullies.

There was this one boy, his name was Pepe Navi. I think we were about thirteen at the time; he was the same age and was a proper little bully who had it right in for our Alfie. Now, as Alfie has said on more than one occasion, if it had been me this Pepe boy was gunning for, Alfie would have just attacked him and had done with it straight away. But Alfie was different from me, he took a bit more time to unleash the fighter in him, but when he did ... fackin' hell, he was a raving lunatic and extremely difficult to stop.

Anyway, we were back at Gran's house, and I was telling her about this Pepe geezer when Gran got a bit annoyed and aggravated, and said: 'Listen, do what my Uncle Bucky showed me: take this peseta in your hand and grip it ... clench it in your fist and never let go of it until the bully is on the deck!' Alfie and I watched, mesmerised and intrigued at the way she put the story over; it seemed as though the coin had power and could turn you into Superman. 'Right, we've got it, Gran,' we hollered. 'Let's see what happens next time the bully-boy shows his face.'

Next day we're on the bus home from school. Alfie had the coin in his hand, clenching it like it was worth a million quid, when up came the bully-boy and he's cursing and making a nuisance of himself. As we sat there, he's stood over us (mainly Alfie) spouting what he was going to do, when suddenly ... BANG ... Alfie has left-hooked him right on his hooter (nose) and it was gushing claret (blood) all over the school bus. Alfie had done him proper with one single shot and he was out cold on the deck of the bus. However, what we hadn't noticed was our little gran (who at some point on our journey had obviously snuck on to the bus) was battering him with her handbag – she wasn't happy: 'You touch my boys and see what happens next time!' she yelled. Gran was off her rocker, talk about Gangsta Gran. Well, what can I say? Alfie and I never got bullied again.

As a youngster Alfie was nuts, and during our childhood he'd shot me, gassed me, strangled me, suffocated me, you name it he did it! But to make sense of his behaviour, in our adult years he has often stated: 'Look Norman, it prepared you for the perilous life that was on the horizon.' And it's true, because, due to my darlin' brother Alfie, and his ruthlessly medieval way of educating me, I never felt the pain others felt, and for that I should thank him … I think! Listen, there are Pepe Navis around every corner, and over the years each and every one of them I've encountered has had a schooling, and for that we say, thanks Granny Bucky, or Granny Cooper. Your education into the whys and wherefores of fist-fighting paid dividends.

Unfortunately, it was time to say goodbye to Spain, which wasn't going to be easy, because, unlike some of the Brits I'd encountered up to this point, most Spaniards seemed to love me, even if it was just because I had the blondest of blond hair, which they oddly referred to as 'Ruby'. Yeah, I could never work that one out either. But anyway, my time in Spain had come to an end; it was obvious I was never going to make a life there, and I needed to chase my destiny, so it was back on a plane to my destination of Aylesbury.

3

STORMIN' BACK TO BLIGHTY

Writers' Note:
Education: who needs it? Well, this boy certainly didn't see it as top-priority, as working hard for a living and bringing in a few quid seemed a far more attainable reality. But was it? Or was this carefree approach to life getting ready to bite him on the arse? Only time would tell...

Right, who was it that convinced me to head home? It was fackin' freezing cold, it felt like I'd moved from the Bahamas to the North Pole as I ran around the streets with my golden-brown skin and shiny white locks, with ice and snow all over the place. I bet everybody thought I was an illegal fackin' immigrant. I was sent to a special school for children with learning difficulties, and this was so difficult for me because at that point in time I was young and was feeling extremely confused. I managed about a year of the Siberian weather in Blighty before slipping back into my globetrotting trainers and heading back to my gran and the luxury of the all-year-round Spanish sun.

Soon after that, and while feeling like I was home again, I started working down the harbour; I used to toss my time away at the fiestas watching bull-runs and carnivals with the locals. However, because of my time away I'd become a bit of an outsider again, and so again I found it a bit of a strain to mix. It was around this time I discovered an inner aggression, I'd had enough of the bully-boys and started to stand my ground, mostly with geezers twice my age and size. But on the upside, when you get used to knocking grown men out, kids your own age become two-a-penny.

For a time, my brother Alfie and me were like a pair of roving adolescents as we went to and fro between Alicante and Aylesbury. Spain, England, Spain, England, Spain ... for fuck's sake, we were like a pair of hoboing tramps. I say tramps 'cos like I said earlier that's exactly how it felt to me ... we had nothing! Sometimes not even the clothes on our backs. Anyway, before too long I was globetrotting again and heading back to the dreary British landscape.

At home I found education a bit of a grind: I learned nothing at school, which was mostly because I didn't understand what they were fackin' talking about; to be truthful, I think I understood the Spanish teachers more than the British ones.

In the winter months it was fackin' freezing cold, which was a far cry from Spanish schools, 'cos over there in December it was still boiling hot, and I got a warm dinner every day. Not to mention the fact that in the morning when I sat down for assembly, everyone would sit three feet away from me like I had the lurgy or something. If I'm honest, it was a bit embarrassing, but eh, that's just the way it was.

I had a few friends in school, but I wasn't what you would call popular. It was a cruel upbringing, but I gritted my teeth and tried to carry on as normal. You see, I didn't know any better and shortly after, while starting to act a little wild, I asked my nan to take me back to Spain, and the toing and froing started all over again.

When I came back from Spain for the last time, I walked into the house and stepped in the front room and I was immediately introduced to a crow and a pigeon flying around my head. I had ferrets, mice and this snake which I lost down the drain one day, it was mayhem; there was no one around controlling us. There was animal shit all over the house, and I used to joke that you had to take your shoes off when you walked out, as opposed to when you came in.

I had a set of scorpion's eyes in my pocket, and I used to play with 'em all the time. I was a proper animal lover when I was a kid, and I used to play with wild rats and wild mice. I was just different to most of the other kids; I was feral. Mind you, on occasion, the little gits would sting and bite me, but it didn't bother me – I still loved them and looked after them.

In 1971, when I was about nine, I was over at this place called Southcourt. Now, back in the 1960s there were some really tough old Irish families about, and one particular bunch were the Fitzsimmons. Anyway, I had a row with one of the boys who was a bit older than me; it was my own fault really, and what was about to happen I probably deserved. 'Cos a few minutes later this boy came back with his big sister: she was about thirteen and she set about me and gave me a right fackin' hiding. She was only a teenager, but she hit me so hard I fell to the floor, at which point she began sticking the boot in. Mind you, I made a right fackin' mistake getting back up, 'cos as soon as I did, she laid into me again and put me straight back on my arse. My face was smothered in blood from where she'd dug her nails in, and she'd also pulled chunks of my hair out. This fackin' Gypsy girl went proper medieval on me. And, up until that day I had never been beaten up. So, broken and a little fackin' embarrassed I went home with my tail between my legs and stupidly showed my gran my war wounds. And while she was seeing to my injuries, she began asking what had happened. I didn't know where to look while I was explaining to her that I had been beaten up by a fackin' girl. But like I say, it was my own fault: I had pushed my luck with her brother, and for that I got a serious spanking.

It was around this time that my uncle moved into a big house down Wendover Road, and we moved into a mobile home at the back of it. For some reason, during wintertime, my uncle disconnected the electric leading from his house to our mobile home; it was fackin' freezing cold, so cold that my fingers and toes felt as though they were about to snap off. The mobile home only had one bedroom, so I slept in the front room with ferrets for company. As you can tell, this wasn't a normal family upbringing by any stretch of the imagination, my mother wasn't around and my father had to work loads of overtime just to keep his mortgage on the house, so for the most part we were parent-less.

It was around this time I started working with Uncle Danny down at Spitalfields Market in Tower Hamlets, in London. This was the first job I'd done after returning home from Spain, although I'd done a bit of work down the port in a harbour over there, so I was used to a bit of graft.

I liked working down the market, because it was an old family way of life: a tradition. You see, the Bucklands are what you call 'fruiters'. What that means is they run fruit stalls ... you know, like the Fowlers do in that *EastEnders* programme on the telly, we sell fruit from big wooden barrows. My grandparents were fruiters, and when my grandad passed away at the tender age of fifty-four, my Uncle Danny took over running them. And over time, he built it up into a little family-run empire, and had fruit stalls all over the place. And, because Spitalfields was one of the biggest and busiest in the country, our family had them in there ... big money spinners you see.

This place was full of the old school lot, you know, big fackin' geezers walking around all moody; most of them looked like fackin' gangsters. I wasn't scared of them, 'cos being from a rough family I was used to it. Although, some of my pals from back home in Aylesbury would have probably shit themselves if they were thrown in the middle of this lot on a cold winter morning in seventies gloomy London. Oh, and I used to sell taties (potatoes) from a barrow on a bit of land for a bloke called Roland Samuels too. This bloke had about an acre of land, and we'd pitch those barrows and do trade from his bit of land. So, again, that was a good few quid in my pocket as well. And, on the odd occasion, I would even take a few mates down the market, and we'd listen with our ears pinned back while all these cockney geezers recalled their favourite tales about the Kray Twins and the London underworld, and I watched as my pals sat with dropped jaws, in awe at hearing these revelations.

My job on the barrows was to fill the lorry up with fruit and veg and carry potato bags from truck to barrow. One thing I learned while humping these heavy bags was that one of the Krays' relatives had a meat stall close to where we used to load up. All the old market people would be squaring up telling people boxing stories; stories that would make your toes curl – I used to love it.

One morning this man was sparked-out cold, right on the floor in front of me. I remember thinking to myself, fackin' hell, this place is a bit lively. What happened was, a milkman had knocked this truck driver out; no one had a clue what it was all about, but, then again, nobody really cared, as it was just the sort of thing that went on down your typical East End workplace.

Now, working part-time and having a few quid in my pocket meant I could pay for my own dinner. It also meant that eventually, I would even have the means to buy my own clothes, and this made a refreshing change from the days when I'd worn the same underpants for six fackin' months. And once I had enough dough to go clobber shopping, I felt like a king as I strutted about in my smart new bib 'n' tucker.

After working down there for a while, it dawned on me that I was only earning about twenty notes a week, still, I suppose at fourteen to seventeen, and with it being 1979 it was probably a decent few quid to be bringing in. Plus, there was the fact that it got me working around a load of grown-up geezers, and this is always good for a young boy, as it settles you right down.

I remember starting work early in the morning and coming through the big trade doors at the side where it fackin' stank of stale piss: not dog piss, no, actual human piss, booze-infused piss from the drunks who probably stood in the doorway on their way home at night, whipped out their old man, and pissed all over the doors – the scruffy old fuckers. Anyway, around this time, I was offered a bit of a promotion.

I was down the Bedgrove Boxing Gym one night and the boxing trainer asked me if I wanted to go to work on the building sites with him doing screeding smoothing a layer of concrete over a surface. I didn't have a fackin' clue what screeding was, but I blagged it a bit and ended up getting good at it. So, that was me, I was in my element, pulling in a ton-plus a week, and now I felt like I was really in the dough.

Working in construction was difficult back then though: there was none of this backing up a big truck, shoving a big hose into the building and spewing the concrete, or the cement and sand mixture, in at the press of a button ... oh, no, no such fackin' luck! You see, back in the day it was all done by what you call hand-ball; you'd load it up by hand into barrows and wheel the heavy fucker wherever the floor-laying geezer wanted it. A lot of the time this would be upstairs, so you would have to load it up onto those big plaster carrying things ... 'ere what do they call them, now? Erm ... hawks, yeah that's it, plastering hawks. Well, you'd have to load the gobbo mix onto this big hawk thing and hoof it all the way up the fackin' stairs. Mind you, it kept you fit, so doing this kind of work, along with the boxing, quickly transformed me into a teenage powerhouse. I didn't have to go down the gym and use the weights to get my bulk built up 'cos I was doing it 'for free' ... on the fackin' building site. I loved it, and the bonus was, it kept me out of trouble for a while.

By the time I was fourteen, I was fighting all the time; I got battered endless times and I ended up with many broken bones, but we were old school and would never grass anyone up. On this particular day my mate Gus got jumped in town by a few boys, so I went looking for them, found them in a toilet, and smashed them to pieces. It was at this point I began to get really aggressive, and I'd had enough of having to work hard to iron out the big tough guys. Alfie and me were boxing by now and were fighting from dusk till dawn; I honestly couldn't tell you how many fights I had, but let's just say I served my apprenticeship. Back then it was non-stop, I'd be working nights, then I'd be grafting down the market early the next morning and back up the boxing gym later.

Believe it or not, I started on the doors when I was about fourteen years of age, as my dad would take me to work with him. Now, some people might find that a bit difficult to believe, but me and my brother had been around these big fackin' men all our lives. Anyway, we started at the Bedgrove Pavilion every Friday and Saturday night. We were only kids and had to wear great big fackin' dicky bow tie things! It felt good though; I felt like one of the boys; one of the geezers. But anyway, I'll give you more detail on that a little later, but first let me tell you a bit more about my boxing exploits.

4

A FIGHTER IN THE ROUGH

Writers' Note

Stormin' Norman was born out of a family of fighters, and the stock he wore this coat of arms for had a reputation that well and truly preceded it. This was an honour that had sailed the seven seas; a coat of fighting arms that had burned its name into the heart of many a far-off land. However, the question was: was pro-boxing a life for him? Did our protagonist have the required tenacity and dedication, or was he simply a fighter in the rough, and due to this, would attaining any such discipline be too mountainous a hill for him to climb?

I started boxing at Aylesbury Boxing Club, which quickly moved to Quarrendon School and was renamed Meadowcroft. As in life, I was always a bit wayward as a boxer. I was a bit of a scrapper: 'head down and smash whatever's in front of you, son,' was always my motto. On the other side of the coin, my brother Alfie had an altogether different mantra. Alfie was always grounded and a lot more technical. He was a counter puncher, and always used it to his advantage, whereas I was a 'dive in and to hell with the fackin' consequences' kind of boxer.

Alfie was like the Mickey Goldmill to my Rocky Balboa (as in the film of that name), but I'm not giving myself praise there, 'cos at times it got me into a whole load of trouble. But hey, I was better than that Balboa geezer anyway, he was a mouthy yank with drum sounds for punches. Listen, when I hit ya I didn't need fackin' sound effects to make it sound painful – the result of the shot itself was always enough.

I've never been one for bravado, and nor has Alfie. At times we were a team, and 'The Buckland Brothers' were well known in that sort of world. As you now know, my brother and I come from a long line of fighters, boxers and scrappers alike, and there were more to speak of, not least that of our other family line, brothers and sisters, the Hardys. So quite obviously, brawling was always going to be a big part of our story.

Alfie always took a different stance to me; as I told you, he was more of a thinker as opposed to my more full-on smash-and-grabber: go in, smash 'em to bits and get out was always my motto, while Alfie would take his time and plan a perfect strategy. He would flag up the whys and wherefores and the best way to execute a set of actions. Alfie and his way of looking at things has always been good for me, and I'm sure that if he had been around at the time I got myself sent to prison, he would have almost definitely steered me away from doing time. Having said that, I really don't think it would have helped because, as I said earlier, at that point in my life I needed to do a stint in the nick; I was in desperate need of some grounding – and when it happened it made me a better man.

My dad was a boxer, he boxed until he was about thirty-four years old, which back in those days was pretty old for a boxer. Dad was also a boxing coach and used to train all the local boys in Aylesbury, and he also ran the Bedgrove Dynamos. Dad loved most sports, and he ran a netball team as well. Like me, Dad was a respected local hard man; he was very quiet and laidback, but when he turned it on, he was tough and uncompromising.

When I was sixteen and a novice boxer, I had a fight with this army man who was a senior up the Civvy. This big fucker was double my age and full of tattoos, it was a close one, but I just inched it. I had loads of amateur fights in my boxing career but hung up the gloves when I was twenty-five years old. Oh, and I did a bit of martial arts during that time as well.

I was terrible with geography, and when I was boxing, travelling up and down the country to fight, I didn't know where places, such as Oxford, were. Of course, I had heard of these places, but I just didn't have a clue which part of the country they were in. I'd been told I was backward, illiterate and a dunce, so I was behind on everything and gave up trying to take stuff in. I used to train on a Sunday afternoon; I'd go right at it and do as many as twenty-six rounds with all my mates. I used to go into fights wanting to kill my opponent and the idea of losing wasn't even on my radar. Boxing is a rough old sport, you have to go in the ring fuelled with a certain killer instinct, 'cos your opponent is there for one reason only, he wants to do a number on you.

My dad, Alfie Senior, was a fantastic coach, and another top coach was a geezer called Pete Garnish. We also had another great coach and match maker called Billy Hutchinson – Bill taught me for years. In his time, Bill had been an ex-RAF combined services champion, so, as many of you will know, he certainly knew his way around a ring.

My brother Alfie used to box for England. Whereas I boxed for the Home Counties, picking up a few ABA titles as I bloomed. I was a light heavyweight, and my brother was a heavyweight and the two of us boxed all over the country. Alfie and I weren't allowed to spar with each other in the gym, because, knowing us well, the coaches there saw it as too dangerous to risk, as we would try and kill each other. Boxing was a fantastic release for me, 'cos with my lack of education it was the only path I could see.

I won a few good medals and still have some of them on display to this day. One in particular has 'Novice ABA Champion N W G Buckland 22-06-1985' engraved on it. I keep some of my old trophies in my barn as a memento of my boxing accolades, and it's nice to look back and remember a particular fight – like a trip back through time, when one second I'm sweeping the barn and the next I'm back scowling and brawling in the ring.

At this point in my life, I was 'doing the doors' (looking after the security for venues such as pubs and nightclubs, including working as a bouncer) regular. Mind you, I never had one of those licence things. See, when I was bouncing, I was often in places on my own, and my way of keeping order was usually down to respect, and geezers having the knowledge that I was one of the hardest fuckers in the area was the thing that stopped most of the violent melees. My brother Alfie and I had been taught to look after doors in the real world from a very young age; we never did any of those poxy courses where they act out all of those soppy made-up scenarios, such as some geezer's got the hump and pisses on the dancing girls, and you have to pretend to talk them down and turn them into a nice guy before the DJ's record stops. No, we had none of that shit: me and Alfie were thrown in at the deep end and there isn't a class on the planet that could teach us the invaluable stuff we learned. You have to get in, dig deep, and forget all about the consequences, and in my book it's the only way, and most of this expertise we picked up from our dad.

Dad was a well-known doorman, he used to work all over Aylesbury. He worked some of the best and busiest places like The Grosvenor and The Crown, and almost every pub and club all over our manor. Dad and my Uncle Chris would often shove us out to work the door: me and my brother Alfie … We were only young, probably about fourteen years old or something.

Talking about my dad, Alfie Senior, for a minute, well, he was another well-respected man. He wasn't a big geezer but fuck me, was he powerful! One bang from the old fella would usually have the fiercest of geezers sleeping like a fackin' baby. Even today people come up to me and tell me how well respected he was. They also mention that apparently he was a true gent: just like yours truly. People still tell me stories about him to this day, and it makes me feel all proud thinking about it.

When Dad took me and Alfie to work with him and it kicked off, he would simply say to my brother, 'Alfie … go and deal with that,' and I would follow my brother over to the trouble and watch his back, and this way I began learning, and would pick up tips and tricks very quickly. However, if the truth be known, we had no choice really, and it never mattered, 'cos we knew we had Dad on hand in case it got a bit too heavy.

Every Friday and Saturday me and my brother would work the Bedgrove Pavilion (now, the Bedgrove Community Centre). We had to wear great big dicky bow ties like the ones my dad and his brothers wore, but it made us feel important – very adult – like we were part of a team. This was all fantastic experience for what was to come, and it taught me very quickly how to sift out the horrible cunts from the nice people. These characters would come in droves and were not nice people to have in your club or pub: idiots like these were out for trouble at any cost, and you had to get hands-on and put a stop to them.

You see, for me, working the doors was like going to school, although a lot more educational, and very quickly I learnt which parts of my artillery were most effective, and I used my skills in whichever way I thought was needed, treating every case on its merits.

Look, if some young runt and his little firm are in one of my clubs and they're causing a bit of a disturbance, and I look over and think I can just huff-n-puff 'em down like a bunch o' porky pigs, I just go over and scream at them: 'What do you want, you want a fackin' row, do ya? … 'cos if you want it, I'll have the fackin' lot o' ya … on your own or all together … it makes no odds to me!' And as quick as a flash they've lost, and probably wet themselves in the fackin' process, and it's as easy as that. Listen, what they don't want is some growling twenty-stone bulldog-looking lunatic with the hump going to work on 'em, so they leave, without a shot being slung.

On the other hand, if a firm comes in who actually do fancy their chances, well then, you've gotta' step it up a gear … show them who's boss; it's a do or die situation and seeing as I ain't the one with booze in me, I'm already a few streets ahead. So, I make my way over … on my own, so already they think I mean business. Listen, this little firm are feared by everybody in town, so, clocking me walking over, looking like I've got the confidence of King fackin' Kong in me bin, already has them on the back foot … at which point The Guv'nor takes over: 'Right, you mouthy cunts, I don't know who you are, and I don't fackin' care, but if you don't tone down the fucking racket (noise), I'm gonna unload every last one of ya … together, or one at a time, it's your choice!'

Immediately, these geezers don't know what to do! They're looking at each other with a look that's saying: 'Is this fucker for real or what?' But they ain't quite brave enough to test me; they know exactly who I am and exactly what I'm capable of, and at this point it's like a game of chess, and it's checkmate and I've just stopped the fackin' clock! And then, knowing they're half beat already, I switch it to 'Mr Nice', and say: 'Look boys, I just want a quiet night, and I imagine you just wanna have a blinding night yourselves. So, if you don't want a row, and ya tone it down a touch, I'll get you a round o' drinks in, and I can go back to my cage unruffled! So, where we at, boys?' I'd ask.

Then suddenly, the mood's gone from aggro to cheery in a heartbeat: and even though I've won this battle of wills, everyone's a winner; The Guv'nor ain't had to get all harassed and sweaty, the landlady's happy as Larry, and this little firm think they've had a result with their newfound friend and a tray full of cheeky free beverages. And that right there is just the way this Guv'nor works.

Ere, I need to shoot back to my teens again, now don't fackin' stick a bad review in because of it, 'cos it's just the way me bonce works.

I was only about sixteen or seventeen when I started looking after people. I remember starting at Friars, where we minded all the bands and groups of that era: Madness, The Damned, Bad Manners, Sham 69, and who's that other group with Mohican haircuts and attitude? … Something to do with a dog … Oh, I know, Bow Wow Wow, they were the fackin' worst of 'em all, although, that singer girl was a right sort, ya know when you look at her properly. But yeah, they were lunatics. They used to smash their dressing room up and we'd be sent up to calm them down.

We also looked after the strippers at the Buck's Nalgo. Looking back, I think I was only about fifteen years old watching 'dropped-jaw' at these birds walking round with everything hanging out. At times I was like a coiled fackin' spring, walking around the place seeing all these scantily clad ladies bending and stretching right there in front of my face. My pent-up frustration could've sent my emotions into overdrive.

Our little firm moved about all over the country, and I worked all over London and London town for years on end. 'Ere, hold up, here's a bit of history for ya: London Town, colloquially known as the Square Mile, is the bit in the middle where all the city's big business is done; the part of the city where all the partygoers hit the night-life, and the West End and Mayfair are where it's at. But less of that, back to the story. Now where was I? Oh yeah, a point I was about to make was … Oh yeah, that's it, how I never brushed shoulders with Lenny McLean on more than just a few occasions will always be a mystery to me, and everybody that knows me. I mean, Stringfellows is just a spit away from the Hippodrome where Lenny minded the door on Cranbourne Street in Charing Cross, and I was often on nights out with the boys over the road at Peter's place: Stringfellows.

On quite a few occasions I'd see McLean when I was out and about. I remember one night as me and my pal Kevin Wilson were moving from door-to-door around Camden, Kevin pointed over to the Camden Palace and said: 'That's

Lenny over there, Norm.' I must say he did look fackin' menacing … ya know … like he was just about to go into battle. Lenny's name was often talked about among the bouncers in the area; they were in awe of the geezer, and for good reason, 'cos let's face it, he was one of the toughest fighters around.

Talking about that neck of the woods for a minute … It was a strange state of affairs down the old Stringfellows and a few other places in the West End etc., 'cos when I used to turn up, the bouncers would never let me in; talk about judging a book by its cover! These judgemental geezers obviously thought I was that much of a lunatic I had no social graces and took it that I would kick off and would be hard to handle if I did. Come on, I know I can be a bit of an animal, but fackin' hell, I know how to hold myself, I ain't some Neanderthal dragging his missus out of his love nest by her hair to take her on a trip up West. Fortunately, during a night out on the town, Tony Hayter (who you'll hear about later) had a word with the 'Big Man' Peter, and from that day forward they left me alone.

Anyway, as I've said many times previously, I'm a kind-natured geezer and my inner lunatic only ever rears its ugly head when someone challenges me. Oh, but don't they fackin' want to challenge me! At times it used to feel like every man and his dog wanted a piece of Stormin' Norman. Listen, whatever happened to mutual respect from one fighter to another? What happened to going about your business and leaving the rats in the alleyways to fight for the scraps? I mean what are we, fackin' dinosaurs or something? Look, I don't want to row with nobody, I just do the job I'm paid for, and, if anyone gets in my way, unfortunately I have to hurt 'em.

Talking about this inner lunatic for a few minutes ... This beast that takes over me from time to time, I don't even know him! And anyway, I don't like the cunt – he's a proper horrible bastard who nobody would like! He's got no morals whatsoever, he's fackin' evil! And when I go way up there in the fluffy-stuff to meet my maker I'm gonna recommend he bars him from entering the pearly gates. Because I'm telling you, if he's in there with me I'm going to bash the fucker to pieces. I'll show him who's boss! I detest him! But he's been with me so long I don't know life without him.

I was a cunt back in the day ... not a shit cunt ... but a cunt all the same. I mean, sometimes before we started work on a certain rave somewhere I would go into the nearest Chinese for a bit of a nosh-up. I'd take the big fackin' dog with me, we'd go inside the place, and he'd drop anchor in the geezer's restaurant or takeaway. The geezer who owned the gaff would go fackin' nuts, then I'd go a bit cranky and rear-up at the poor fucker; the geezer was only protecting his place, but I didn't give two-fucks. Look, at times, I just wasn't a nice bloke. I had a lack of morals, and I put it down to depression. But hey, I ain't using that as an excuse, I was horrible, and I have no one else to blame but myself.

Fortunately, with my new-found life, peacefully sane and calming, I've managed to separate myself from the lunatic. I've put him away in a box marked with a blood-drenched cross and a slogan saying: 'DO NOT OPEN AT ANY COST' – and I'm safe. He leaves me alone to live my life, and that for me is beautiful – as beautiful as the serenity in life that my wife Nanette the peacekeeper introduced me to. Anyway, back to yesteryear...

So, we were working in Bow one night; we had a good team of men with us and it was coming to the end of the night. Out of nowhere the biggest geezer you've ever seen, who was definitely 'on something' started larging it up. He had these black leather gloves on, you know, the ones you see most doormen wearing and believe me they can fucking hurt. And with this man's frame one shot on the chin and it could have been game over. Anyway, there he was, as large as life, dancing about on the spot and moving his hands in all these weird positions and I'm looking at him thinking who the fuck's this? Wacko fackin' Jacko or something? He's got these two other big lumps with him as well; I'd never seen them before either and they were egging things on and also getting a bit rowdy. Turns out he was the head doorman of a club over in the West End called Browns or something. He then started acting up and shouting stuff like: 'This is my manor … my gaff,' while pulling his mates all over the place and falling onto them. And all the time I was looking at his shoulders and thinking they're higher than my fackin' head, he was colossal. With that, our security team began to surround him, and my pal Kevin Wilson picked up a bottle and I remember thinking, 'Fackin' hell, son … you're going to need a stepladder to get up there and hit him on the head.'

Seconds later, the man said, 'Look here you lot, I'm the man, and I want a cut of this fucking place tonight!' At this point all the boys on our firm were looking over at Alfie, waiting for him to give them the nod to spring into action. But my brother Alfie is as sharp as a tack, I could see he was holding out, 'cos he knew it was only words and bravado at that point. Then finally, I had seen enough, and up stepped the beast. 'You fackin' want some, you big fucking ape? You come round here lording it up, thinking you're the fucking big man … you're a cunt … you're a cunt, do you want a fackin' row?' I screamed at him. Suddenly Alfie spoke, 'Take him outside Norm,' he said, 'cos he knew I was ready to blow. (Incidentally, I don't know how true it is but the boys reckoned that because he was so big, he'd had the front seat taken out of his BMW and he sat in the back to drive, and I could believe that.) Anyway, out he came with his firm trailing behind him. Adding to the bravado, one of his mates had taken his top off and was tensing his chest muscles out, giving it the large one. For me this was like something out of a comic book, all that machismo bollocks is just child's play to me, and I began screaming at them again, 'I'm going to rip you apart ya cunt! You fackin' want it, do ya?' Suddenly, they all lined up in a row, and Alfie said, 'Norman, over here!' and with that we turned on our heels, walked back inside the club, and shut the doors. We were laughing inside, and they were left out in the cold like a bunch of fackin' idiots.

Eh, let me tell you about another good pal of mine, Chris Gallop. Fackin' hell we've had some mad times together. I've known him since my mid teens, so you can imagine the sort of lunacy we've got up to over the years. During the days of the 'Skins' (skinheads), we used to meet up in a local boozer called The Two Brewers. Back then in the early 1980s, we were a proper couple of liberty takers; we used to go down the Brewers and help ourselves to whatever tipple we fancied from behind the bar – we were a right pair of cheeky fuckers.

This was back in the days when my old man was active; Dad had a big name back then and was well respected as a fighter. It was around this time when he set up his own security company, he looked after loads of boozers and was the manager of the massive Agora Shopping Centre. I was head geezer to the rest of the lumps, and Chris worked all over the place with us. Dad used to send us down the pubs and clubs that employed him, and we'd clean the places right up; well, most times it was after a load of tear-ups and a right load of heartache, but we got the job done and everyone was happy.

I remember one New Year's Eve; the night was going fantastic with no trouble at all. Then suddenly, in what seemed like a heartbeat, it switched when a group of tooled-up geezers turned up full of agg (aggression) and attitude. It's always the fackin' same, always out for making a name for themselves, and for what? Anyway, I wasted no time at all and told them they weren't coming in, then, seconds later, it went off like a dam busting.

In the madness and mayhem, I spotted this one lunatic going at it like a crazy fucker with a bar. Anyway, I swooped in a bit lively and took the bit of metal from the cunt and done both his kneecaps: he was screaming like a banshee, and that was him out of next year's marathon. It was like the Wild West in the place, some poor fucker who was just a barman even lost an eye, these animals didn't give a fuck. But it was like that back then – it was the norm. People turned up with knifes, hammers, guns, and all-sorts. Some of these tossers must have thought it was sixty-minute makeover the amount of 'Do-It-Yourself' artillery they were carrying. If I'm honest, during really bad periods you would be fighting for people's lives.

Another night down the Agora it went off and this stupid lot pulled out a load of Samurai swords! Us fellas weren't tooled up, we never were, well not at that point in time anyway. Mind you, we soon learnt how to sniff out the bad bastards who needed a bit of proper retribution, from the ones who just deserved a bit of a backhander. The Samurai lot got a proper spanking; we taught them how not to think the odds were on their side – fackin' animals – and they call bouncers animals! The world's gone fackin' loopy.

Having said that, we were a bit fackin' loopy ourselves. One time when we were leaving the Agora, we took a bit of a detour. Now, remember, there was a whole army of us, there must have been about five car loads altogether: five cars bursting at the seams looking like that fackin' *Ant Hill Mob* from the cartoon of the 1970s. Anyway, on our way home, we went round all the back roads, through the villages and past the farms and that, we'd usually stay in the motors and enjoy the scenery, but this one night we all decided to jump out the motors and nick a load of hay-bales. We then set them alight in the road and sped off back to Aylesbury all innocent. It was fackin' nuts! Mind you, I did try and stop them … 'cos deep down I was a good boy … do you believe that?

Talking about villages…

I remember one night when our firm had about four dos on round the manor on the same night, and one particular do was full of skinheads who apparently were spoiling for a row. So, our boys down there got on the radios and rounded up all of our boys from all the other places. And when they all turned up it was a sight to see. We strolled into an image of these skinheads playing up hell while repeatedly singing, 'Bring on the bouncers, bring on the bouncers, bring on, bring on, bring on…' Well, you get the idea. Anyway, you can imagine the silence when they looked up and saw our boys there in force. Strangely enough, they eased up with the audition for the *X-Factor* and everything went back to being nice and peaceful.

'Ere, here's a valid point I'd like to make you all aware of…

The Old Bill might have slagged us off behind closed doors. You know, when they have to be respectful in front of their governors at the annual Christmas dinner-dance, and they're making out they abide by the laws of the land. Well, that's all done to be teacher's pet and impress their bosses, but back in the real world, on the street where it's fackin' dangerous, these fuckers used our little firm as back-up on more than just a few occasions. Listen, they used to come over the Agora and beg us to help them sort problems out over the pubs that were adjacent – things they just couldn't handle. And, as always, we'd step up and sort their problems out. Strange though 'cos we sorted rucks out for them many times, but this one time the headline in the paper the next day read: 'Aylesbury thugs take Milton Keynes!' Cheeky fuckers! We were helping out the police; we were helping them keep the peace. I must say though, through all the violence and misdemeanours at our gentle little hands, the Ol' Bill never lifted any of us once, any accounts of violence just seemed to get washed away with last night's doner kebab wrappers. And too fackin' right – ya know? You scratch my back…

The Bedford skinheads were a big problem back then, and coachloads of the fuckers would turn up and run amok all over the town, dishing out blood and threats to anyone and everyone. It unnerved a lot of people and probably left them a bit frightened to go out of a night. These 'apparent' neo-Nazi geezers even ran amok in Woolworths; a fackin' retail outlet was all it was, and these animals were running wild, frightening the punters and staff every weekend. So, Chris and the boys on the firm brought me in; I think they needed to fight fire with a fackin' inferno, and they knew I was the man to do it.

Apart from fighting with the Skins, I also used to knock about with them, too, and to be honest most of them were good people. I mean, yeah, you got the odd glue- and bag-head who was off his fackin' trolley and wanted to fight the world, but those ones got a quick seeing to and quickly jumped back in their pram. There was this girl at the time, bit of a tomboy; I think there was quite a few of them back in the day. These girls wore all the same clobber as the geezers but on the downside, they'd often get mistaken for a fella, and, I might add, often got set upon like one.

I remember this one girl called Kelly something … yeah, that was it, Sue Kelly, I think her name was. Well, she was one of these types of girls. Well, this one night I walked round this corner and these nutty skinheads were kicking seven-shades of shit out of her: they were battering her as if she was a geezer. Anyway, she was screaming and hollering for her life; you could hear by the tone of her voice that she was a girl, but that little detail wasn't of any concern to these animals – they didn't seem to give two fucks.

So, anyway, I've steamed in and I'm growling at them Gypsy style. 'Leave the mort (woman) alone … chavvies!' I shouted (chavvies, meaning 'son' in Romany speak). Well, this was a bit of a dig at them, as I was belittling them by calling them a bunch of fackin' kids. Anyway, I told them not to push it; I told them that if they stopped beating on her, I'd leave it there and say no more about it. And luckily enough they saw sense and calmed down. A little while later, I heard that earlier on in the day they'd been kicking off with the Old Bill, so they were obviously out looking for someone to bully. Years later I bumped into Sue, and she said she believed I'd saved her life that day, and without over-egging my part and coming over like Billy Big Bollocks, I'd say she was right. 'Cos, seconds before I turned up, they were about to give her a proper hiding.

Back then we had about sixty geezers on Dad's payroll; sixty lumps with the hump if ever anyone got in our way, and me, Chris Gallop, Stefan Wilson, Barry Bennett, and my brother Alfie were at the top of that tree. We dished out beatings to anyone who wanted it, and when people came to me with a problem (which was an everyday occurrence) I'd deal with it on my own, or ten-handed if they happened to be some dirty, good-for-nuffin' tooled-up bastards.

You see that's the way it always was, and that's the way it's always been. And that right there, my friends, is the sole reason I'm forever on guard. Listen, I trust my friends until they become untrustworthy. I help my friends until they become dependent on me, and I'll bully the bully until one day he becomes the bullied. I can't help it, and I will never make excuses for it – it's just me and it's how I choose to be.

5

RISE OF THE GUV'NOR

Writers' Note

Our man ruled over places like thunder in a force 9 storm. That didn't mean he set about people for no good reason. No, Norman's way of ruling was a little different to most, as the man had a hidden talent ... a hidden gem in his flesh 'n' blood armoury. And this my dear reader was his voice! Our man's voice rattled the parquet and shook off the roof of every establishment he minded. Thus shaking and quaking the life out of the troublemakers.

My name was getting about all over the place, apparently people were mentioning my name all over London, regarding the work I was doing for a fella called Charlie Bear, mainly the work I was doing at a place called WKD, and, because of this, people who wanted their places looking after started enquiring about me too, at which point my phone started ringing more and more.

Shortly after, I started getting calls to go into places round Kentish Town and Camden and all around those areas. So, my name (like Lenny McLean's) was doing most of the work for me, so if people knew I looked after a certain place, they would think twice about playing up in there, and at this point in time, this sort of hands-off bouncing was sought after. I mean yeah, it stopped the violence, but it also stopped the Ol' Bill having to get involved after someone had taken a heavy hiding.

I was obviously still working locally, and one night while working down the Berni Inn, Barry 'BK' Bennett came in; you've heard me talk about Barry, but just so you know a little bit more about him, Barry was a welterweight boxer of good pedigree – a great boxer he was as well, and, back then, he sparred over at the Thomas A Becket with a lot of the top names of the day including Nigel Benn, Terry Marsh, and the late Gary Mason.

Anyway, Barry and this other geezer (who I didn't know at the time), Peter Salange, came into the place; I said my hellos, and then took myself off to the toilet. A few minutes later after buckling myself up and leaving the bog, I walked out and there was fackin' murders going on. So, I asked Barry what was happening, and he told me that his pal was the geezer fighting with some of my boys.

With that, I've rushed in to break it up when suddenly Barry's smashed me in the chops, so I told him, if he did it again, I'd have to fackin' hurt him, but he didn't listen and hit me again. Barry was then fighting with the rest of the boys when he caught me (this time accidentally) with a shot AGAIN! Well, that did it, and I hit him on the chin, and he flew over the fackin' bar. Somehow, the lot of us who were involved in the tear-up ended up on the cobbles outside, at which point Barry was then asking me what the fuck was going on? So, I told him it was his mate who had caused all the agg. Anyway, Barry grabbed his pal Peter and they've fucked off down the road leaving me to calm the fackin' mayhem down that his mate had caused.

The following day (in the hope of getting this little fracas sorted out) I rounded up the boys and took them over to the Civic Centre to meet Barry and his mates. The place was packed with his lot and our lot. (I bet the punters there thought there was a march on or something.) But we kept it so it was all nice and amicable and sat down like fackin' businessmen and ironed out the rough spots: Barry knew it was his pal who had kicked it all off and apologised on his behalf. There was another problem on the horizon though. In my haste to sort this shit out, I'd forgotten to inform the rest of the boys who turned up on the following Sunday, down the Lobster Pot (Chinese Restaurant) looking for Barry and his mates. Anyway, I think it went tits up as Barry ended up ironing a few of them out, that was until I got word out to them to forget all about it. But anyway, everything soon went back to being nice, and once again we were all back to being good pals watching each other's backs from that day to this – great man Barry, a fantastic sparring partner – fackin' hell, that geezer is another who knows his way around a ring.

Back in the 1980s I worked the clubs and pubs on my own. This was simply down to the way I'd do things. I guess it was unique, probably old-school, but in my day, I was the only one doing it. I could stop trouble before it started, and on many occasions I have walked into the toilets and heard a geezer telling his pal that he liked coming in places that Stormin' Norman works 'cos he's The Guv'nor and there's never any trouble in the places he works. But like I say, this was all down to the way I worked. One thing I learned very quickly was that if a geezer was acting up and I wanted to calm him down without too much agg, I'd lift him up off his feet and he would instantly become putty in my hands; especially if I smashed his head into the fackin' ceiling; it probably made him feel like he'd already lost the battle, and this show of my overpowering strength, had done the trick. I suppose it's because I had made him feel weak, as if I was picking a baby up from out of its pram. His defences would have all been neutralised, and he'd give up trying to fight.

In about 1986, I met Dave Courtney. I remember that year well 'cos it was the same year that Lenny McLean done a number on that mad Gypsy geezer, and it had been all over the ten o'clock news. Dave was a friend of Lenny's, and along with many other familiar faces Dave was well-known, well-liked, and his name and reputation seemed worthy enough for me to get myself wrapped around him a bit – so I did.

Having only been pals for a short while he called me up and asked if I wanted to go on a bit of work with him – he said it would pull in a nice few quid, saying, 'There's a grand in it for you, and it will only take us about ten minutes.' Then he went on to say, 'Listen, it'll be easy if you're on the firm.' And, I was in, a thousand notes for the time it takes me to have a shower, yeah, I'll have some of that, I thought. So, the following day we met up over in Hackney, in a café called Yummy's, I think it was, and chatted over a cuppa and a Danish while he filled me in on the bit of business. Now, I won't take you through our conversation, 'cos Dave will say I've got it all wrong, so I'll just explain what happened instead.

Guess what? Yeah, you got it: it was on a Gypsy camp. Fackin' hell, does anyone except me like going on a Gypsy camp? 'Cos usually, as soon as you mention the word Gypsy, most geezers get all windy and bolt. Well not me, I was brought up with them and I know how they tick. I also know how to speak to them, which can be a huge plus point; that is if having a chinwag is needed, but from what Dave told me in Yummy's, I didn't think there would be a whole lot of rabbiting going on. The next day, we arrived at the camp about six, as I'd told Dave previously that it was better to catch 'em half asleep with their dick in their hands, as they'd probably be in a dream world and not ready for a barny, let alone a fackin' tear-up.

So, we parked up a lane about a quarter of a mile away and took up the rest of the hike on foot. The ground was a bit wet and muddy, so we were trekking through sludge, shit, and all sorts on our way through this field. Luckily enough, I had my big boots on, but Dave, the soppy fucker, he had a pair of white loafers on – well, they were white when we first got going, but after about two steps they were as black as Newgate's fackin' knocker.

Anyway, we kept going and ended up at the back of this camp; there was no one about so we slipped through the fence and found the caravan we were looking for. We knew it was the right one because it had a black goat tied to the gas bottles. Having a bit of a nous with animals, I raised my hand to pat it on the head and the fackin' thing bit me. 'Argh ya cunt!' I yelled, as Dave immediately tried to shush me. 'You saw the cunt bite me, Dave,' I said, 'the bastard fing must have fackin' rabies or something!' Dave shook his head and said, 'Well that's woken the cunt hasn't it, Norm?' So saying, he pointed towards the window where you could see a shadowy figure moving. 'Now, let the fucker off its leash.' I shrugged as if to say, why? And he said, 'Just do as I say, Norm … you'll see what I mean in a few seconds!' So, I did what he told me, Dave smacked the facker on the arse, and off it ran like a greyhound on speed, through the caravans.

'Ere, remind me about greyhounds in a bit.

With that, the geezer came running out with a bar in his hand and ran off in pursuit of his AWOL (Absent Without Leave) Billy. Me and Dave quickly whipped inside his gaff and grabbed the case of dough (cash) we'd come for. Fortunately, it was out on the Formica worktop looking like he'd been counting it out ready to divvy up to his cronies. And with that we fucked off – no agg, no witnesses, and I earned enough dough for a nice little holiday. Mind you, I'll think twice about patting a goat on the head next fackin' time!

Like I say, he's sound-as-a-pound is Dave, but on occasion he lets his mouth run away with him, and he does things that people might deem a little fackin' naughty. One time he did a little something on my manor and I weren't too happy, so I drove over to Plumstead to have a little word. When I arrived at Camelot Castle, Dave was nowhere to be seen; he must have heard through the underworld drum-beating that I had the hump and decided to slip away for a bit while I calmed myself down. Dave knows only too well how I operate, and also knows that when my head goes there's no talking to me, but when I've had a few hours to calm down I'm back to being Mr Placid. He isn't soppy in the head, Dave, 'cos he was right, and later we spoke about the incident and ironed out the rough spots amicably. I'd never want to fall out with him 'cos he's a good man and has never used me once. Plenty of others have, but never Dave – he's a diamond.

Right, what was I going to say about greyhounds? Oh yeah, that's it, the dog track ... 'ere get on this.

I was in London one day doing a quote with Alfie for a bit of security work when my phone went, it was Dave. 'Norm ... You busy me old mate? 'Cos if not I need you to come

down the dogs with me … I've got a bit of a retrieval job on!'
Initially, I told him nah, fuck that Dave, saying that he knows
I hate those cunts who have dogs ripping each other's jaws
off, and that I'll end up ending some cunt if I see anything
like that. But he told me, 'No Norm … I mean down the
greyhound track, on my patch!' 'Oh, alright,' I said, 'why
didn't you just fackin' say that then? Anyway, what time you
picking me up?' He told me he'd come for me at seven that
evening and filled me in on the detail. ''Ere Norm … can
you wear a dark suit?' he asked. Oh, fuck that, I thought, I
hate wearing a whistle (whistle and flute – suit) on a job … it
makes me feel all hemmed in and that. But then I thought,
well, he must have a good reason, so I pulled out my best bib
and tucker and waited for him to arrive, and ten minutes
later I heard a horn beeping outside...

'Who's the tart?' I hollered as I jumped in, spotting a bird
done up like a dog's dinner on the back seat. 'You hear that,
Chantelle?' Dave said. 'This big lump just called you a prossy
(Prostitute)!' And BOSH, she's hit me with her fackin' purse
thing. It must have had a gun in it 'cos it weighed a ton and
almost took my fackin' ear'ole off. I screamed at her and told
her I was only having a laugh, and that I actually thought she
looked lovely, and was just geeing her up for the journey. She
immediately went soft and said, 'Aww … sorry Norman, I
thought you was coming the cunt like his other idiot mates!'
I told her, no, I love women and I'd never be horrible to 'em.
'You ask my missus,' I said, appealing to her better nature.
Anyway, we forgot all about it and laughed all the way there.
Dave couldn't stop laughing as he kept saying I'd been done
by a bird, and that he was there to witness it. I remember
thinking: it wouldn't be the first fackin' time. Remember the
Gypsy girl from earlier who I told you gave me a good beating?

Shortly after, we arrived at the Marshes dog track, we jumped out the motor and made our way over to the tradesmen's entrance, as Dave calls it. The plan was for Chantelle to pull some toff who'd done Dave's pal out of 50k (£50,000) and rumble him; the problem was that he always had a few meatheads with him, and Dave wanted me about in case it got a bit lively. So, with that, Dave fucked off and spoke to this other geezer who apparently was on the firm with us; there were a few of Dave's mob plotted about just to even up the odds.

Chantelle went off and did her stuff. Her job was to give the geezer the come-on, get him all boozed-up with champagne and that, then flirt and talk all seductive with him until he was ready to pop, then, coax him back to his place with the promise of taking things a little further. (Well, that's what he would be hoping!) Then, I'd take care of the meatheads (making sure they didn't follow Dave) while Dave followed the toff and his new bit of skirt home, then Dave would terrify him 'till he handed over the bit of dough he owed.

Next thing I know, as they're leaving with Dave on their shirt-tails, some big mouthy Brummy (from Birmingham) cunt (who was one of the toff's minders) grabs Dave by his collar and tries to put a block on him. Immediately, I've swooped in and smashed him with a right-hander straight to the temple and he's gone down like a ton of bricks – he was out cold. Suddenly Dave hollered, 'See to him,' and wasted no time catching up with the toff to follow them back to his gaff.

From this point I never had a clue what went on. I talked the minder round, got him a drink and said that I'd seen some cheeky cunt hit him from behind and run off. The big fucker was shaking his head, baffled, but didn't question me. Which I was pleased about 'cos I couldn't understand a single word he was fackin' saying. With that, I slipped off and got myself home. I only found out what had happened when Dave turned up the next day with a bag of dough for me. Apparently, the toff was that scared he handed over the fifty large and then slung five more on top in exchange for the promise of no reprisals from Dave's associates. I got two bags from that little number, nice bit of work for a quiet Sunday. I did ask Dave why he'd asked me to wear a fackin' suit and he said he didn't want me turning up in a big white suit wearing loads of leery tom (tomfoolery – jewellery). Because, he said, it would draw attention to us. Cheeky cunt, especially coming from a geezer who went down the Old Bailey dressed like a fackin' medieval jester.

Strange thing was, a few years later I ended up working with the Brummy minder on one of Vic Bellamy's merchandise events. He recognised me straight away and said, you were the geezer who helped me out over Plumstead. He said, he'd ditch the job with his governor 'cos he found out there was a hit out on him, and he didn't want to get caught up in the crossfire. He said, he didn't give a fuck for the governor geezer anyway, because he was stitching up all the wrong faces and the chances of him getting taken out at some point was totally expected. I never told him the truth about that night down the dogs, but if he reads this, I imagine he'll twig a bit sharpish.

6

WHO PUT THE AGG IN AGORA?

Writers' Note

A retail arcade is a place of safety, yes? Well, not according to our protagonist it isn't. For this place was a playground to fuel war; it was a site for settling gangland disputes. Well, at least that's what the ruffians believed it to be, that was until our man Stormin' Norman sat in the governor's chair.

I've always got on well with people, and even more so the older I've got; I imagine I'm a little bit wiser and a lot more tolerant these days. I show people respect and they treat me respectfully in return. You see, it's not always about violence, as my good friend Henry 'H' Simpson will tell you. One day I was doing security in a shopping arcade in Wolverton called the Agora; I often met up with Henry there, and we'd have a bit of breakfast and a good old chinwag – ya know, we'd set the world to rights. Then, once we'd eaten, we would walk around the upper-level chatting and enjoying the odd joke or two.

A little while later as the place got busy, it would get difficult for me to walk ten yards without being stopped by old ladies, children and even younger women who would all greet me with a big hug and a kiss. I'd always talk to anyone and take the time to listen to their many stories about anything and everything. Some would talk to me about starting school, a new job, a house, or whatever else, and I would show them I was keen to listen, interested, and would always ask the right questions that would hopefully make 'em feel good about themselves.

I've watched children excitedly running up to me with drawings they had done in school and sometimes they would even have drawings they had done of me, and I would always be laughing or giving them my big lion-like roar that everyone loved so much. Some would even roar back at me, thinking I was some big tame lion; unbeknown to them, underneath lurked a raving lunatic waiting to be unleashed, but I'd have been devastated if ever they had to see it. To the little ones I was just a big bear, and some kids would hold my hand and walk along with their arms around my waist – me on one side and their mum on the other.

To the young ones, I think I was such a big-hearted man, I was well liked, and they all remember me for being responsible for clearing out the unruly and unwanted, who had previously run riot around the Agora and almost made it a no-go area. We used to do a lot for the waif and stray kids – you know, the naughty ones. Around this time, we had seen some ex-professional boxer from Watford working with the kids, he was putting them on the straight and narrow and we thought, we'll have a piece of that and sort of copied what he was doing. We had the Old Bill's backing, which was good, and because of this we opened a boxing gym in Aylesbury and had about twenty kids as members, coming along on a regular basis. I remember this one woman saying: 'Good luck with them ... you'll need it ... they're all animals!'

These kids were aged between twelve and sixteen, most of 'em had ADHD (attention deficit hyperactivity disorder) and other issues, but I never thought for one minute that they were animals: these kids just needed a bit of guidance, a bit of nurturing and a helping hand.

We did this for a good six months and when they'd won a fight, we had ex-professional boxer Herol Graham present them with awards for what they had achieved – their little faces would light up; you'd swear they had won the lottery. By this time, the club was getting really busy, and I used to take them all on pads (these are the protective guards worn by a training partner on the hands or arms, allowing the trainee to punch hard without doing damage). There was loads of 'em, some were little rascals with learning difficulties, but they all took a liking to me, and I used to spend time with them all and talk to their parents and give them feedback on how their little ones had been performing.

When I was working down the Agora, part of my job was to look out for people nicking stuff. Well, this woman used to come in, and I always followed her about and kept my eye on her. Anyway, I think she got the wind up and told her husband, and the next thing you know she turned up with her old man in tow. He made his wife stay where she was, then walked over to have a word with me, saying that he had to talk to me because his missus was getting edgy 'cos I was watching her every move and she felt uneasy at the thought of me thinking she was pinching stuff. So I assured him that that wasn't the case; he looked at me all baffled, until I told him that I was eyeing her up; I said I was only looking at her 'cos she was so fackin' hot! I told him she was that much of a sort I couldn't take my eyes off her.

Well, he walked off, told his bird what the score was, and she immediately burst out laughing; she probably felt a bit embarrassed at the thought of it. But listen, this was just my way of turning a bad situation into something good. That girl probably went off home thinking she was the bee's fackin' knees – and I hope she did – I like the idea of people (especially women) feeling good about themselves. It makes my day. Like I have mentioned previously, I was punished for being slow as a kid and I always promised myself that I'd help out kids who were similar to me.

This was the same down the boxing club. I mean, just the look and size of me would usually intimidate them, not to mention the booming of my voice. But once they got to know me and bonded with me, everything was fantastic, mind you they didn't take the piss; they knew not to step out of line. When I took 'em on the pads in the ring I used to take a bit of a dive and pretend they had hurt me, but then, some of the little gits would catch me with a shot by mistake. To me this was great – it boosted their confidence. I just enjoyed seeing them smiling; it was a tonic.

You have to remember, many of these kids had been bullied, but fortunately the work we did with them gave them a bit of courage; courage enough to belt the shit out of me. God knows how many times I've stood there taking body punches from them. I'd mess about and go down on the canvas, and our jobbing 'ref' would count me out as if they had KO'd me, and immediately, they'd be standing over me thinking they'd just knocked out the heavyweight champion of the world! They must've felt like Rocky Balboa. I loved it – I had a lot of time for them all, and at times it made my dangerous life worth living.

As I said earlier, I've always got on great with people and because of this I became a well-known figure in the Agora.

I was like the everyday Santa Claus without the big beard and toys to give away. Many young girls who I have known since they were kids would often bring me pictures, and then show me their homework and exam results; you could see how proud they were because they were beaming from ear-to-ear. I would always make a fuss of them, just like they were my own children. I believe I was loved and respected by them all and, as they got older, some would call in to the Agora to show me their new hairstyles or their clothes; I felt like a long-lost uncle they'd only just met. Sometimes their mums would turn up for a bit of advice and a chat, and I'd always make myself available and listen to their worries etc.

For some reason, one day I got a bit of a niggle and suspected that one of these girls was being abused by her boyfriend. So, me being me, I asked her outright, but unfortunately she denied it. Strangely enough, I often thought the geezer she was with seemed a bit funny, 'cos he always kept his distance. My motto has always been: never trust a man who will never show his fackin' face. Anyway, I wasn't fackin' happy and told her I'd be keeping my eye on the situation.

A week or two went by and I hadn't seen sight nor sound of the girl, and again, I thought something was a bit off, 'specially 'cos she usually called in to see me once or twice a week. Anyway, feeling a bit suspicious I called my pal Henry, gave him the full SP (the complete background story) and told him that I'd have to take a trip round the house to see her mum and hopefully find out what the fuck was going on; unfortunately, when I got there, she wasn't in.

The following day me and Henry were having some breakfast when the girl's daughter (who must've only been about four) came running straight up to me in the café and she was crying her eyes out. I gave her a big hug and said,

'What's up darlin'? Tell your Uncle Norman what's been happening.' The toddler was sobbing so much she was struggling to get her words out, and because she was so young, I knew, or should I say hoped, that her mother wouldn't be far away. Suddenly, through the snot and tears, the toddler managed to cry out that David, her mum's boyfriend, had been pushing her mummy around and said that her mummy was bleeding. I knew it; I was fackin' furious, so immediately, I asked her where her mummy was, and, while still crying, she managed to splutter out, 'She's on the square, Norman!' Now, the square she was talking about was on the outside of the Agora at the back of the shopping centre, across a small road. So we had to go looking for her, and also had to take the little girl with us.

At this point I picked up the child, who was still crying, poor little baby, then me and Henry left our food and rushed straight outside to find her mummy. When we got to the square, there was her mum sat down with her head in her lap. So, I walked over and lifted her head, noticing immediately that her face was all puffed up and she had swollen eyes, and looked like she'd had a big bust-up. And then it came; the red mist was starting to overcome me, and I said quietly through gritted teeth, 'Right, who's fackin' done this?' And, through the tears and stuttering she said, 'Honest Norm, he didn't mean it ... it was my fault!' And I was thinking to myself, 'How the fuck is it your fault? No man should hit a woman ... especially in front of their kids.' With that, I immediately passed the toddler to Henry and off I went to find the no-good wife-beating fucker and sort him out, and guaranteed I was gonna make sure he never hit another woman again.

So, I'm mooching around the place with the hump when I spotted the bullying bastard going into a slot machines arcade. With that, I marched in, barged straight through the rabble. I've then grabbed the cunt by the scruff of the neck and dragged him across the road over to where the little girl's mum was sitting: 'Look at what you've done you no-good cunt!' I snarled, while calling him some other choice names in the process, yet all the time keeping my voice down low so as not to scare the poor frightened little baby girl.

Anyway, I thought to myself, this cunt needs to be taught a lesson, so I lifted his arm right up above his head and made the evil bastard stand there while I was twisting his arm round as though he was a rag doll. By this point the lad was in agony and started shouting to his pals who had followed us out of the arcade, to come over and help him. One brave one started swearing and shouted at me to let him go. I don't know if he knew his mate had just bashed his girlfriend's face in, but I thought, he must do, so if he comes any closer, he's going to get it as well. I noticed the baby girl looking over, she must have been frightened out of her wits, so I started to move the geezer around as though we were dancing and said to the toddler, 'Look sweetheart … Dave's dancing … everything's okay, so don't get upset, little one!' And with that I dropped his arm and with a quick shot I sneakily smashed him straight in the face so that the little one couldn't see it, and then I pulled his arm back up his back again; he was wincing in pain, and I thought, well, that'll teach you won't it, you bully-boy cunt.

My pal Henry was still there, so I turned to him and said, 'Stay with the girls, Henry, do a few magic tricks or something and make them happy while I'm gone. I'll be back in a bit!' I guided this Dave, who was like a puppet on a string, over to his mates who were still giving it Billy Big Bollocks, yelling and gesturing at me, so I started growling back at them,

'Right you brave mouthy cunts … what the fuck are you lot going to do? This bastard has just beaten his girlfriend up right in front of her little daughter, and you lot think that's okay, do you? Do you cunts think that's a good thing to do … do ya? Well, fackin' do ya?'

By now I was in a full-on rage, and I was screaming at them, 'C'mon you bunch of wankers … come on … I'll have all of you!' I was getting more and more fackin' infuriated as I spoke, 'I'll tell you what I'll do, I'll hang onto this cunt and take you lot on with my free hand … come on, who wants to go fackin' first?' Quickly, his mob of no-hopers began to back off. So, I dropped the bully's arm but smashed him in the head once again for good luck and shouted, 'This is who you should be pissed off with! You should all be ashamed of this low-life … now fuck off the lot of you … you fackin' disgust me!'

Immediately, I clocked two of them and realised I knew their mums and said, 'Right, I know who you are; wait until I tell your mums on Saturday when they come down the market! Sticking up for your so-called mate who's just beaten his girlfriend up in front of her baby daughter. Go on, fuck off, you make me fucking sick!' Then, with that, the lot of them slipped away like little rats. I gave this Dave another slap and told him to fuck off out of my face, and he ran off and followed his pals with his tail between his legs – dirty rotten bastard. Next time I'll really fackin' hurt him, I said to myself as he slipped off down an alleyway.

I made my way back to the mum and the little girl, who by this time were smiling due to Henry and his warm and loving personality. I told the girl to go back to her mum's house and stay there, but I also said if that wasn't up for grabs, I would let her stay at one of my flats, I told her she could have that for a few weeks 'till she got her life in order. Thankfully, she agreed, and went back to live with her mum. She got a new job babysitting and I made her check in with me every Saturday to make sure things were okay. That little girl is now in her twenties and I'm glad to say she is still a good friend of mine. As for her mum, well eventually, she got herself a new partner and she marched him over to see me to get my approval. I was happy, as I could see how much happier she was, so I gave her the nod and they are still together to this day.

Now, taking on the job of security at the Agora wasn't the walk in the park I'd imagined it to be, fackin' far from it. Apparently, they had been having quite a lot of beef in there and the place was going to the dogs. You see, before I took over, there had just been the obligatory uniformed run-of-the-mill security geezers looking after the place, and to be brutally honest most of them were fackin' useless. Some of these geezers had been warned off by the minions from the local gangs, and with violent threats becoming a regular thing, the security boys became a bit fearful: they just couldn't handle the job. Anyway, due to the above mentioned, I was called in. Apparently, the uniformed bunch left the Agora in shit-street and no other company had the balls or the right manpower to step in and clean the place up. However, this is me we're talking about, and I love a fackin' challenge! Plus, there was the fact that I was in between jobs at the time, which meant this little number was the absolute bollocks. Also, I was friends with a girl who worked in the Agora Café, and she filled me in on the whys and wherefores and gave me the heads up on who exactly these troublemakers were.

Now, I was used to going into places and trying to clean them up, but with the continuous gang fights in the area this one was probably going to be my hardest challenge to date. There were a lot of wannabe gangsters about at the time – each of them trying to prove they were the toughest boys in town. Well, I thought to myself, not on my fackin' watch!

A few days went by, and a meet was set up for me to have a sit-down with the owners of the Agora. So, their original plan had been to employ three geezers, however, after seeing me and the way I put myself over, they decided that I could do it on my own, and I was over the moon and thinking, good choice son, you know it makes sense. And that was that. Just a few days later I was brought in to rid the shopping centre of its rats, making it a safer place for the shoppers and their families to visit. I mean, these people were getting scared, and you don't expect your granny to be frightened while she's doing her weekly fackin' shopping, now do you?

Basically, what was happening was this. There were two rival gangs, and although these little fuckers were only about eighteen years old, some of these boys were big lumps and most of 'em were tooled up and could be very fackin' dangerous. But for me, this was the only life I knew; cleaning up the streets had become part of my daily vocation. And anyway, at the end of the day I had mouths to feed.

The full SP was that these gangs were trying to take over Wolverton, and the area around the shopping centre had quickly become their main ground; this seemed to be neutral territory, and anywhere else on the manor would have meant that one of the gangs were playing away from home. According to my eyes and ears on the street these lunatics were using the shopping centre café and open areas to meet up and plan what they were going to do next. To me this was a bit of a shame, because most of these boys knew each other, but their family rivalries were totally taking over, and all just for pride and to gain a little control. As I said, the shoppers had become terrified, and the shop owners (all small businesses) were losing money right, left and centre. And if the shop owners dared to say anything they were threatened with extreme violence, and it had all gotten right out of control. These boys needed a new direction, and I was the geezer to put it in place. Fuck off out of it or you're going to get hurt, was soon to become the Agora's new USP (Unique Selling Point), and hopefully it would very quickly bring many shoppers back to a place where, once again, they would feel safe and completely at ease.

Shortly after, I started the job and brought my own style into the place and, slowly but surely, I moved most of the fackin' lunatics out, but at the same time I managed to draw a few over to my way of thinking and made friends with them in the process. Now, it was obvious to me that it wasn't completely over with the ones I had sifted off out of the gaff, because I found out I had banned a few of their older brothers from various places in the past, so they instantly took a dislike to me. These boys wanted retribution and were apparently on their way to put me in my place.

At this point it was clear to see that I had a bit of graft on my hands and the threats were coming in thick and fast, but like I always say to cunts issuing threats: 'Listen, you lousy cunts … don't say it, fackin' do it!' Anyway, one morning I was doing my usual patrols around the upper level of the shopping centre and I spotted a gang of these fuckers heading towards me. Now, as I said previously, these boys were no mugs and some of them were big fuckers, and the next thing ya know they started to surround me. Having been in these situations many times I knew I had to box clever, and my first thought was: get your back up against the wall

Norm, 'cos the last thing I wanted was some cheeky fucker swooping up behind me and sticking a cheeky shot in my nut from the back. But that wasn't about to happen, because the position I'd got myself settled in, even being outnumbered I could still see every last one of these mugs. I relaxed myself a bit and kept my hands down by my side, ready to strike like a cornered viper and prepared to take a few of them out in the first explosion. My brain was working fackin' overtime as I was scanning them all, making sure none of the cunts were tooled-up (carrying weapons), and from a quick scan I could see that some of them had lumps of wood, and at least two of these wankers had what looked like long screwdrivers. Still, I remained calm and tried to talk them down; I began politely asking them to leave it, and to calm themselves down and just leave.

I glanced up towards the stairway and could see my mate Henry strolling up from downstairs; he had obviously heard some sort of commotion and had come upstairs to investigate. Henry isn't your run-of-the-mill streetfighter, but listen, he runs around with Lenny and the like, so when I say he can hold his hands up a bit, I'm sure you know exactly what I'm talking about, and knowing this, I knew he had my back, especially seeing that he was behind them, and they weren't aware of it.

This gang were giving it the big one, so I said to them: 'Listen boys, get yourselves down my gym later, and I'll fight you one at a time … or if you want it, I'll fight the whole fucking lot of you at once in the ring and out of the way of any witnesses.' I was still calm, but you could clearly hear the aggression creeping its way into my voice – the beast was on his way out, and once he'd reared his ugly fackin' mug there would be no way of stopping him. Mind you, I still had a job to do to get them all out, so I said, 'Right, c'mon boys … enough is enough … you've just got to go!' Suddenly, the one closest to me said the fatal words that I really didn't want to hear: 'Yeah, and you and what fackin' army is going to make us leave?' And unbeknown to these wankers, that right there was the only trigger I needed. There was no fackin' way I was being pushed around like all the previous guards, so that was that! And, with one BANG – one smash to his stupid fackin' bonce, the mouthy cunt sank to his knees and rolled onto the floor, half dead. Well, the rest of the wankers couldn't believe what they had just witnessed; they looked petrified and were mumbling to themselves.

At this point I bent down and picked the lad up from the floor; I gave the mug a look of disgust and said to the others: 'Aww look fellas … he's pissed his fackin' pants … now take this cunt home to his mummy so she can change his fackin' nappy!' However, halfway through the sentence I grabbed this other big fucker around his neck and growled while spitting and snarling, 'Right, look here you bunch of cunts … my tea is getting fackin' cold, so fuck off before I really lose my rag, and we'll call it a day!' But, unfortunately by this point the beast was in full voice, and I began screaming and taunting them to make a move.

With that, one of the boys (who had a baseball bat behind his back) tried to raise his arm, so I grabbed the bat and smashed him across the elbow with it, as his pals just looked on in total shock. I then said to another one of the wankers, 'Oi, hold this fackin' bat!' And as he reached out to take it from me, I tapped him on the chin with the back of my hand that was holding the bat, and he hit the ground with a thunderous clap. The beast in me then began screaming again, 'Now then you fackin' cunts, if you don't want to end up like these couple of wankers, or worse, I suggest you make your way out of here … NOW!' I was furious, and if in that moment they hadn't retreated, I would've gone into full blown lunatic mode, and even I didn't want that to happen, 'cos when he steps out from the shadows, no fucker is safe.

I stepped forward, roaring again, grabbed one of the lads and hurled him at the rest of 'em, and as they slowly began to back away from me, I roared even louder. Then suddenly, there was peace; everything settled down and I shouted over to my pal, "Ere 'Enry … show this fackin' lot out the door downstairs please … before I really fackin' lose it with 'em?' I carried on shouting and bawling at them, and not one of them would look into my face; they were just looking at Henry with their tails between their legs and their heads down. I watched them as they walked down the stairs and out of the ground floor exit; they looked like a flock of sheep spared from slaughter. As they were leaving Henry made them hand over their tools, apparently saying that if they didn't hand them over to him, Norm would come looking for them.

The above incident simply highlights that in my world I could have no fear. I know it seems a bit crazy at times but that kind of situation and everything that went with it is the reason I earned the title: The Guv'nor. Because as was always the case back then, whenever I stepped into the breach, I always made sure I sorted out the shit. The story with those boys was this. Apparently, it was all part of a gang war that had gotten out of control and led to a few boys getting stabbed up, and apparently there had been at least one murder as a result. Anyway, after that day of unholy retribution I never had another problem with their top fellas and their soppy little gangs. And from that day forward I kept the place yob- and hassle-free, not to mention reducing the shoplifting. You see because most people had ultimate respect for me, thieving became almost non-existent. I had succeeded in my quest to rid the place of its rats, and I was happy to say that the place was 95 per cent free of all its problems.

After the battle, I had just joined Henry back in the café for a cup of tea when this little girl came running in. She was upset and was struggling to sit on my knee. Her mother ran in and told me that the little girl was worried and had made her come back to see if I was okay after what had gone on with the naughty men. Her mum went on to tell me that the little girl had refused to get on the bus until she had come back to the Agora to check on me. And I said, 'Look darlin', I'm alright … it was just a little game me and those boys were playing!' I gave her a massive bear-hug and she smiled, said her goodbyes and went off as happy as anything. As they walked away, I heard the little girl's mum say, 'See, I told you Norman was okay.' It upsets me a little, because when I go into the zone of that beast, I blank out and I don't have a clue who is around me. As I've said earlier, the Beast is a law unto himself. And if I'm honest, at times he even fackin' frightens me. To make light of what had just happened, Henry said while laughing, 'Well Norm, I suppose you handled that nicely.' I just looked at him smiling and said, 'Well yeah, that's all well and good me' ol' mate … but by the time I got back, my fackin' tea was freezing cold!' We always have to make a joke after a bad situation, it helps settle the mind.

At around this time, I had a few properties in and around the area, and I used to let them out to people in need. The only problem was, I was too nice and used to let them all stay on, even if they couldn't afford to pay their rent; I felt sorry for 'em, I've always been like that. The last thing I wanted to do was chuck them out on the street and in the gutter. I ain't like these horrible bastards you see on the TV who would chuck an old granny out in the snow on Christmas Eve. See, I do have a heart. But, as is usually the case, some of them people would ruin it for the others by taking my kindness for weakness and would take advantage of my kind nature. It was clear to see who were the ones who were taking the piss. But listen, I gave them plenty of warnings, but being selfish they ignored them and that's when I would have to step it up and give them a 'proper' final warning. Then immediately, most of these mickey takers would leave of their own accord. I honestly don't know what would have happened if they hadn't left nicely, but knowing the way I am, they'd probably still be living there now.

I was re-letting this one property as the old tenants had just moved out. I had some new tenants waiting to move in, so I told them it would be ready in the next couple of days as I needed time to get it all shipshape. So, before I handed over the keys, I went round to the house to do a bit of a check, and fuck me, when I got there, I opened the door, and it was in a right fackin' state. Immediately, I got a few mates in to help me get the place cleaned up. We painted some of the rooms and worked through the night, and made it look decent for the new tenants to move in to.

I checked all the electrical appliances: they were okay, well, all except the cooker, as two of the hobs had gone on the blink. So me and my mate dragged it outside onto the path and phoned a dealer to collect it and replace it with a new one. Anyway, it turned out that the dealer was flat-out busy and did not have a suitable second-hand one in stock, but it was Christmas at the time, so it was obvious that they would be desperate for a cooker; can't have Christmas Day without a turkey… it's against the fackin' law, isn't it? Anyway, I rushed all around town looking for a replacement, but due to it being the festive season all the second-hand shops in the area had sold most of their stock and didn't have anything worth buying. I tried everywhere, and all to no avail. Completely pissed off with the toing and froing, I popped into the Agora café for a quick breakfast, and as luck would have it my good pal Henry was in there, so I said to him, 'I've looked everywhere, Henry … I can't let these tenants down, definitely not at this time of year, but I've even tried buying a new one, which was all going great, until they told me they couldn't deliver till after Christmas. Fackin' hell Henry, I'm down a dead-end road, what can I do?'

Well, Henry and I were sat there for a while, racking our brains while I mopped up the last of my breakfast with a nice half a loaf of bread and butter, when suddenly my phone started to ring, and on the other end of the blower were the new tenants. I looked at Henry, pointing to my phone and said, 'Oh shit, it's them, Henry … I guarantee it! I bet they want to know about the fackin' cooker!' Anyway, I answered the phone and this geezer on the other end said, 'Norm, don't bother with a cooker, we've found one on the path outside the flat! Anyway, we've dragged it inside and would you believe it, it fits like a fackin' glove!' And I replied, 'Okay son, are you sure?' and he said, 'Yeah, of course Norm, two of the hobs on it don't work, but that doesn't matter … it will get us over Christmas, and it'll also save you a good few bob!' I immediately hung up, took a gulp of tea, turned to Henry, and with a big grin on my face I burst out laughing – you couldn't make this fucker up … now, could you?

IT WAS THE ONE WE'D SLUNG OUT EARLIER! Fackin' hell, I thought I'd landed smack-bang in the middle of a 1970s comedy show.

As I hope you know by now, I have always tried to be kind to people. I mean yes, I can be a lunatic when I want to be, but for the most part I'm gentle and caring and I like to make everybody feel special; it costs nothing to be like that, so why go out of your way to make somebody else's life worse? Life is hard enough as it is without anyone adding to people's woes.

I had a sparring session one time with a geezer called Lukie 'Boy' Milligan; this boy was a double amputee, mind you, but the way he moved around a boxing ring you wouldn't know it. Lukie boxed on the same bill as the Stormin' Norman title match under the ABO (Adaptive Boxing Organisation) rules and was matched up against Bryan Leaver, who is also an amputee. It's at times like this, while working with geezers with insurmountable problems, that we very quickly realise how much we take life for granted. And how everything handed to us at birth we take for granted: walking, talking, and perhaps even the simple art of communicating. And watching these young boys going at it, full of power, driven by sheer will and determination in the terrifying confines of a boxing ring, gives me fackin' goose bumps – it really does. Also, these boys never seem to piss and moan, they just accept their lot, move on and get on with life.

Talk about living life against adversity, well, anyone who went into the downstairs Agora Café a few years ago would have seen the general manager, and this fella was someone who had walked it, lived it, and worn the fackin' T-shirt; this little geezer always had his eye on the ball; he was a right stickler for time and arrived bang on the dot every fackin' morning dressed up to the nines in his blazer and well-pressed trousers. This little geezer would turn up, proudly carrying his little briefcase for all to see. The man's hair was always neat and tidy … well swept back, very smart, and no matter what the weather, he would be making himself busy smiling at everybody as they passed by him, and without fail he'd shout over to everyone and they'd always holler back: 'Good morning Walter.'

Walter was a vertically challenged geezer. This little fella was only five foot and a fag-paper tall, but he wasn't fackin' shy, this boy had the character and confidence of a giant. Every day without fail, Walter would make his way over to his table – mind you, you'd be bang in trouble if you dared to sit in his seat, 'cos this was his own little place of safety; this was the director's seat and this man's little domain. Anyway, once he got his arse on his seat, he'd open up his briefcase, take out a clean fresh white apron, an apron that would appear to the onlooker (given his height) to be a bit long for him, and he would put it on carefully, smoothing it out as it went down his front. Then, as pleased as punch, he would pull out his baseball cap (which had the title 'General Manager' printed on it) and stick it on his noddle (head). Then he'd quickly stand to attention, go over to the counter, order his special drink of strawberry milkshake, and quietly sit scanning his empire. You see, in Walter's world he was the king of the Agora, and this plastic café chair was his throne. Now, if you haven't already worked it out, our boy Walter was a little different from the rest of us. For our man Walter had Down's Syndrome – but shush … don't tell him I told you that or he'll come after me.

Walter's job (although he was never actually employed by the owners) was to clear the tables of the day-to-day café debris, a job that only he was allowed to do, and you'd be in deep fackin' trouble if you ever tried to clear your own … he would do his fackin' nut!

Walter adored me, and I him, and every day at bang on the dot, according to his 007, James Bond wristwatch, you would see him constantly checking his timepiece while mouthing my name to people, expecting them to explain why I wasn't down for breakfast, and, without fail, this little pantomime would be played out every single morning. And once we were together, I'd tease him and roar at him: 'Who's The Guv'nor? … Walter is!' And he fackin' loved it! And he would beam from ear-to-ear as proud as could be – bless him.

Sometimes, due to his condition and for no reason whatsoever, Walter would suddenly stand still, with horror splashed across his face and he'd be shivering, crying, and rushing around on the spot in sheer panic. And then, just as suddenly, he would make his way to the café's stockroom and wedge himself tightly into a dark corner, petrified and crying. Walter was scared shitless about something that no fucker else could see. It was heart-breaking to see.

At this point in time, I had my own office above the café, and at times like this I would get a call to come down, and, knowing how distressed he'd be, I would immediately drop whatever I was doing and make my way down to the stockroom. Once I got there, so as not to frighten him any more, I'd quietly walk in, find somewhere to sit close by him, and I'd very gently start talking to him, and try to calm him down. Then, for as long as it took, me and the little man would be in there until he was settled. Then, I'd take him back into the café, get us both a drink of his favourite 'Pink Stuff', and we'd chat at the table for as long as it took to lighten his mood. And once I'd brought him fully round, we'd sit, and laugh at the top of our lungs for everyone to hear.

Due to his disabilities, Walter was completely set in his ways, and everything had to go according to his little plan, and part of that plan was to stride endlessly down the corridor that led up to my office, waiting to see me, and if there was no sign of me, he would go to the front of the café and look up at the upper level where my office was and whisper my name. (I don't know why he did this: perhaps he thought he could summon me if he whispered.) Anyway, once he'd spotted me, he would quickly go back to his table and sit, all excited, waiting.

As soon as I got down to him, I would not look at him once, I'd simply go directly to the counter and order his food, and then, I'd act all silly and dumb, scanning the room as though I was looking for a table. Then, suddenly, I'd hear him, in that unique tone, shouting: 'Norman, come here… Norman, I've saved you a seat!' I would wind him up though, and say, 'Sorry son, I didn't see you there, but okay, I'll join ya.' And Walter's face would be beaming, he'd be so happy, and we'd be chattering about goodness knows what the whole time. I'd always tell him stories and give him a big 'GUV'NOR' style roar, and there he would stand, in fits of laughter.

Once we had finished our food, Walter would proudly clear the plates, and when I got up to leave, once again, I would roar my 'GUV'NOR' roar at him, and tell him that he'd better behave, OR ELSE! Walter fackin' loved this and would reply by doing a strong-man pose with his arms in the air and his muscles all flexed up. And if anybody was looking over at us, he would brag proudly to them that he was my friend … bless him. It makes me all choked up inside to even think about him. This was a daily ritual; he was so happy to tell everyone that I was his pal, and every time he caught a glimpse of me, he would rush up and give me a great big, massive hug, and would have to be persuaded to let me go! I loved that little man to pieces – what a man – he's worth ten of me. And in my eyes, Walter will forever be the real Guv'nor!

Sadly, as time went on, Walter visited less and less, and when he did visit, he usually had two or three carers with him, and with every visit you could see a difference in him. If I wasn't there, he would get in a bit of a strop and another mate of mine Henry Simpson (my surrogate step-dad, who helped me in my 'minding' duties) would sit with him and do magic tricks for him. Walter loved Henry to pieces as well.

One day when Henry was doing magic tricks for him, he made a salt pot vanish. Walter looked on, all shocked and amazed, then looked at the person behind the counter to see if she knew what had happened to it. Then, before he'd had time to blink, the pot was back on the table. Walter was totally confused (mind you, so was I) and hadn't a clue what had just fackin' happened.

The following day I was sitting there with Walter and suddenly he put his hand over one of the salt pots and said, 'GONE!' I tried to act all confused, as if I'd never seen it before, then suddenly he pulled his hand away from it, but it was still fackin' there – Walter was pissed off a treat! I think he thought Henry was a fackin' magician or something.

One day I was sat in my office when I spotted Henry escorting a very old looking Walter to the cafe. I knew something was wrong because his hair wasn't combed right, and he didn't look as smart as he usually did. He also looked a bit down in the dumps. Holding back the tears I popped out to see them. Walter gave me a huge hug and just clung to me, saying nothing for what seemed like a lifetime. After a while, his carers would turn up and say that Walter had to get back to his home. Both carers looked at me and shook their heads as they tried gently to persuade Walter to let me go. Then, suddenly, the old Walter appeared, and he thrust his hands out in front of Henry and said, 'Henry … Gone!' Hoping with all of his heart that he was a wizard too, and that he'd made Henry disappear. Then quickly, he turned to me mouthing his name and began raising his arms in his famous muscle-man pose, shouting the loudest roar he had ever done. Then Henry and I stood silent and watched him leave, and never looked away for a second until he was out of sight. It was a sad day, because I think we both knew that that day would probably be the last time he'd visit.

About a month later (on a day he would usually be at the Agora) he failed to turn up for work. Someone made enquires and found out that he had dementia; dementia that had been brought on by his condition and the medication he was taking. Apparently, it had all become too difficult for him, and he wasn't coping. Then, a short while after that, we were given the sad news that he had passed away quietly in his bed. According to sources close to him, he had been well looked after by a skilled team of nurses and carers, who had stayed with him and comforted him right to the very end.

The news of Walter's passing left us all totally devastated, and from that day forward and for a long while after, not a soul sat at Walter's table, and the roar that we shared together took a long time to return. I always felt like I could have done more, but Henry says that I was always there for Walter and says that I gave him the gift of my friendship and that was all he ever wanted. And if I'm honest, I think our 'Enry is right.

Because during his short life, we kept Walter in good spirits, and when Walter was scared and upset, I was always there to save him. Well, all I can say is this: I hope that those things are all true, and I hope that lovely man's life was at least a little bit better for knowing me.

7

THE 'MADNESS' OF KING NORM

Writers' Note

Our man has laughed, cried, and at times struggled to get by. And with the PTSD he must have suffered after certain traumatic events, he needed a release; he was in desperate need of some conjured-up activity that would take him out of the dark world and mayhem for a spell. Often this came while he was standing at a door, as our gangster-come-prankster injected his own way of casting a rainbow over the murky world of 'Minding the door'.

I done a lot of years on the doors with a great friend of mine, Vince, Vince Day to give his full name. He won't mind me mentioning his surname but I have to be a bit careful 'cos he's a bit of a high-flyer these days; he's left the streets behind for the comfy warmth of an office, sorting out people's money deals and what-have-you. But, like I say, back in the 1980s he worked with me and we had some lively and funny nights while minding the doors.

Vince was a tasty bastard, good with the gloves on, so much so that I trained him up in boxing, teaching him tricks that I'd picked up over the years. Mind you he'd never fight me, I know this 'cos I asked him once, while we were stood outside on a cold winter's evening. ''Ere, Vince my old son,' I said, 'if there was anyone around you'd rather not go toe-to-toe on the pavement with, who would it be?' And without a second to think about it, he replied, 'You, Norm … fucking you!' So, anyway I said, 'Why's that then, my mate?' And with that he said quite adamantly, ''Cos you're a fucking lunatic!'

I remember one night, me and Vince were looking after this place and I'd planned a little prank on him. It went like this: Vince was always going on about the number of birds he pulled, the amount of chicks he could entice into his coop, so I thought, right, I'll have you for that, Vince boy.

The following night I arranged for this DHL wagon to roll up with a special delivery. At the time, Vince and I were tucked up getting a bit of warmth inside the boozer and I said, 'There's a delivery for ya mate, you'd better go out and sign for it.' He did that and then asked if I'd give him a hand in with it 'cos apparently it was a bit awkward to carry. Next thing you know we've shunted it inside the club and Vince is pointing to it saying, 'Norm, it's moving … what the fuck is it?' Well, I'm stood looking dumb as fuck, shaking my head and he's looking worried. 'Well, it ain't going to open itself … open it up son,' I said. 'Yeah, but it might be a snake,' he answered. 'I'm sure I can hear it fucking hissing!' And I said, 'Hissing? You're fackin' hearing things, mate … just open the fucker up and see.' And with that he peeled open one of the flaps at the side and shitloads of chickens came hopping out and started running all around the club. 'You cunt, Norm,' he shouts, and I hollered back, 'Well you said you've got dozens of chicks on the go … well they're all grown up now and I just wanted to reacquaint you with them!' Well we laughed the fackin' roof off the place. Mind you, we had a right game getting 'em back in the box, they were on the dance-floor and all over the shop.

Hindsight can be a fackin' horrible thing! At times it can work in your favour, but mostly it can be a right ball-ache. Well, ball-ache is a little too generous, sometimes it can give you the right raving hump; sometimes it can almost ruin a part of your life forever. What happened was this…

It was late … I'd just finished up down the club, I'd said my goodbyes to the staff and on my way over to my motor I was mopping up the stragglers from outside. Suddenly, a geezer shouted over saying some other geezer was picking a fight with his pal. Oh, for fuck's sake, I thought to myself, as I followed him over to these two geezers who were about to have a ruck. Anyway, one was a big fucker and the other was a skinny little runt and the big geezer has the little one by the scruff of his jacket. 'Here, hold up!' I said, to the big lump. 'Let go of him, mate … he's only a bit of a kid!' And as I went to gently put my hand on his shoulder, whoosh, he's swung a right-hander at me … and BANG, I've smashed him with an uppercut to his jaw and he's asleep in a standing position. Okay, so it was a bit of a heavy shot, but listen, this big gorilla was trying to take my fackin' head off.

Then, as I was helping the big geezer up from the gravel I whispered to the little fella, 'Go on son, get in ya' taxi and fuck off out of it … I'll sort the gorilla out,' as I steadied the gorilla to his feet. ''Ere big man, sit yourself down here,' I said, pointing to a set of steps behind him. 'You must've come over a bit funny pal, 'cos one minute you were on ya' pins (legs) and then suddenly you've gone down like a ton of bricks – do ya feel a bit queasy, my old mate?'

Dazed and a little confused, the big geezer said, 'I don't know what happened … My head went a bit wobbly, and that was the last thing I remember. Has someone spiked me lager or something?' I told him: 'Probably mate, we get all sorts of jokers in here, you'll have to watch yourself next time you're down the club. Here, let me get you to a taxi.' I was chatting to him as I motioned to a cab driver to help me put him in the back of his motor. 'Look after him for me, would you mate?' I said to the cabbie as I walked away to get in my own car. Right, I thought, now I can get myself home! If it ain't one fackin' thing, I said to myself through gritted teeth as I started the engine. So, I'm on my way home, and singing to myself on the way, imagining what I was going to shove down me funnel (throat) when I got myself back to my nest.

Anyway, about two minutes away from where I live, still fantasising about my beef sarnie, I spotted a load of flames coming from a Gypsy camp; it looked heavy and out of control because the smoke looked like it was coming from a fackin' power-station chimney, and with that, I spun off down the lane to have a butcher's (butcher's hook – look) for myself.

Fuck me, right in the heart of the camp, in the middle of a load of caravans, this other caravan was up in flames, and there were gas bottles all over the shop – enough gas cylinders to blow up the whole camp! Quickly, I jumped from my motor and ran straight towards the flames. It put the wind up me a bit, 'cos I remember thinking to myself, if it's this fackin' hot where I'm parked (which was about twenty yards away), what's it going to be like when I get closer? However, thinking there might be kids inside the caravan I didn't give a fuck, and off I headed, straight into the flames.

As I ran up, I noticed the woman who I guessed was the mother was screaming: 'My babies! My babies!' So I hollered at her, 'Are there kids in there? Are the fackin' kids in there?' I screamed at the top of my lungs to anyone who was listening. 'Oh, fuck this!' I mumbled to myself as I began to kick in the door.

It was no good, the door wasn't budging. So I ran round to the window at the back; the caravan was boiling hot – it was like a furnace, so hot in fact I could actually feel the burn on my face. I remember thinking as I got closer, this heat I'm feeling is from the outside, so fuck knows what it is going to be like when I get in there. And I'm ripping at the metal-framed widows, attempting to loosen the edges so I can climb through. I couldn't hear any noise coming from inside, but you wouldn't, would you? I thought to myself, you wouldn't be able to hear the faint voices of children above the noise of the fire and flames, not to mention all the people around screaming. But of course I was kidding myself, wasn't I? Of course you'd be able to hear the sound of kids screaming, but it didn't stop me, even with my hands burning, I just kept on ripping at the metal.

Anyway, I'd just managed to pull the window out when a big whoosh of smoke and flames almost took my head off. I must have looked like one of the black-and-white minstrels (a now politically unacceptable old TV programme where white singers were made up to look like black people) as I wiped the soot from my eyes and mouth. But I was in: the metal had given way to my strength. As I clambered through the gap where the window had been, the flames took over (later a fireman told me that as soon as the air met the flames it would've gone right up). And it was over – I couldn't move another inch, the smoke had filled up my lungs and I was beat! It was the only fight I'd ever lost, and I would've willingly given up all my past wins just to triumph in this one. I mean that, no win, whether in the ring or out, was ever more important than saving that little girl. And in that moment, my life changed forever … I was heartbroken. It's a memory that would haunt me for the rest of my days. And resonating around my head, from that day to this was: 'Don't be too hard on ya'self, Guv … you tried your fackin' best!' The trouble was, I never actually believed that, and in my heart and in my head, I never will!

I received a commendation for that; the police paraded me about like some fackin' hero; they gave me a piece of paper as a reward. It didn't make me feel any better though, that poor little baby had her whole life in front of her, and I've got a piece of paper as evidence … a document that is simply a reminder to me of a battle I lost; the detailing in ink of what could've been. And all the time it echoes around my head: if I hadn't stopped to help those troublemakers outside the club that little baby would still be about. Hindsight eh? It can't half be a killer!

Weeks later I was speaking to a friend; I was still very upset that I hadn't been able to save anyone, and it was really getting to me. And I knew that only the passing of time would help me feel less sad about it. Word had spread far and wide across the Gypsy community, it had even travelled as far down as Stow and Appleby Horse Fair.

Looking back, I remember in the mayhem as the nightmare was unfolding right in front of my eyes at the Gypsy camp, the Old Bill turning up, and all the Gypsies were hurling bricks at 'em. Well, a little while after there was an enquiry into the incident and a few of these Gypsy boys ended up getting prosecuted for manslaughter. What had happened was that the Gypsies, believing the caravan to be empty, parked their cars against the door and set light to it and it went up like a forest fire; this was all down to some family feud (as is usually the case with travellers). But listen, travellers are extremely family orientated. Travellers are so driven by family values that if they knew a child was in there, no way would they have set it on fire. That sort of thing goes against everything they believe and live for. I'm sure that throughout the rawness of the whole thing the victim's family members would never pay credence to this. But I would hope that in the fullness of time they would see this was the truth. However, that's easy to say when it's not one of your own. It was a terrible day, and something that will stay in me bonce forever.

When I was on the firm with my brother, I was a bit wild! Alfie used to say I was a loose cannon and I suppose he was right; I just didn't give a fuck! Alfie used to say I reminded him of that Chopper bloke from Down Under (the crime drama films featuring Mark 'Chopper' Read), 'cos like me, he said, people would cut him up and batter him and he would just keep on fighting.

Due to my 'loose-cannon' attitude, back in the day when we were doing the doors, Alfie would stand me right at the back and watch over me from a distance. I don't know what he thought I was going to do, I mean, I was just doing my job – the job of keeping your children safe. And if I spotted some little runt way up at the front and he looked to be concealing a blade or something similar, I'd quickly swoop up a bit lively, I'd do a bit of growling and take whatever weapon he had from him. It was as simple as that. Listen, if I never did things like that, that tool may have ended up stuck in one of your own kid's lungs, and you'd probably never see him or her again. So, all-in-all, I imagine that'd sit well with you, knowing the job I was doing was keeping your kith and kin away from harm.

Sometimes, when it was quiet, I'd watch on as one of the other bouncers tried to mimic the way I did things, and two seconds later they'd be stabbed-up, cut-up and on the pavement crying for someone to help 'em. Look, I had my own way of going to work, and I guess my ferocious way simply terrified 'em out o' their wits, and if that means it stopped some likely knife killer from doing his worst, then I'm happy with my actions.

You see, back in the day I didn't give a fuck for my own safety, but to be quite truthful I never have. Even to this day, I only seem to care what happens to others. Look, I was paid to do a job of protection and that's what I done. And at fifty-eight years old and strong, if you slipped me on the door to look after your money and ya' business, I'd do the same as I did back then; two attacks to me heart and a stroke, yet I'd still wade in like a fackin' lunatic with nine lives – it's just the way I'm built, and it's simply the way my head works. Now, I'm not trying to make out I was indestructible … I just never considered the outcome.

A job came in working with a good mate of mine who today, God rest his soul, is no longer with us.

My pal was only forty-six years old when he had to have a heart-bypass and unfortunately he didn't pull through, God bless you, sir. Anyway, before all this sadness, the two of us had to go on a little trip over to Benidorm to do a job that turned out to be a right fackin' nightmare. We caught a plane and got ourselves out to Alicante (my old playground). Once there, we had to hire a car (a car, I might add, that was so small that it turned out to be fit only for Snow White's little helper geezers) and make our way to Benidorm before finally arriving in Casa Eladia.

According to my pal, we were there because some gang had been threatening the man we were working for. And apparently, he was fearing for the safety of his wife and children – fucking scumbags they were, coming it strong with someone's babies, I thought. But hold ya' horses, it turned out we were actually on the wrong side of the fackin' battle! According to the word on the street, the gang making all the threats were actually the good ones, 'cos it turns out the geezer we were supposed to be protecting was ripping off the supposed wrong-uns, or 'pirates' as he'd referred to them. It's lucky we found out when we did, or we may well have ended up in fackin' body bags over this load of shit.

Anyway, this all came to light one evening when one of these geezers said to me, 'Look what's in that boot?' To which I replied quite abruptly, 'Look, son, I don't give two fucks what's in the boot.' But, to my astonishment, when he flipped open the lid of the boot there lay a right little fackin' arsenal of guns; it looked like they'd raided Rambo's fackin' gun cabinet. And after sorting it all out we headed back to our rooms – still alive and unscathed – well apart from my wallet ... that took a bit of a hammering.

When I had come back from Spain the last time, when I was about fourteen years old, this kid came back with me. This geezer was from Morocco – we got on well and he interested me with his stories of this rough place called Sidi Bazar. Anyway, years later I've gone over there for a few weeks with my mate Steffen Wilson. Now, this man could have a row, he's a proper tasty fucker! He's been shot that many times I think he's got lead running through his veins. And when he does get shot, he just gets back up and chases them off. Steffen has been shot in his legs, his back, fackin' everywhere ... the boy's a machine! I'd done a bit of time with him in poky (prison) in the past, and one day when I was stood in the queue for the phone, he would saunter past myself and the others without a care in the fackin' world, and people would say, 'Are you going to say anything, Norm?' And I'd say, 'No ... course not, he's a fackin' mate of mine.' He was a right fucker, just to wind the screws up he'd grab me, all aggressive like, and start whispering to me while pointing over at the screws. He loved winding them up – it was his way of putting the fear into them.

So, where the fuck was I? Oh yeah, Morocco! Me, Steffen, Barrie, and a few others arrived there off the train and immediately some row kicked off over taxis, and because of this, none of the cab drivers would take us anywhere. But then, suddenly, I found one that would and climbed in; this fackin' motor was tiny, and because I took up two seats the cheeky fucker wanted to charge me double. It was night-time and late and there were no lights in the taxi and the windows wouldn't even open, it was a right shit-tip. So, we get to Sidi Bazar and could see about twenty men with machetes having a go at a man on his own, he looked like he had taken a right pasting, 'cos his face was covered in fackin' blood. So, my first reaction was to stop the car to help him, but the taxi man was desperate to leave it and drive on; to be honest even Steff said we should keep going. Anyway, it turned out it was a local drug dealer from another town who had stabbed one of the locals in the arse. Apparently, they tortured him for a few days before handing him over to the police. Well, all I can say is, you play with fire...

After this little bit of lunacy, we took ourselves into this café for a coffee where they would put weed (cannabis) in the shisha pipe. Well, Barrie (who we used to call Mike Tyson) had a blow of it, but it was too strong for him, and he immediately started coughing. Then a few minutes later he started to sweat: he was sweating like a chav on dole day. What the fuck was in it I don't know, but Barrie was in a bad way and got all paranoid and took himself off for a walk on his own; he was gone about an hour, and we started to get a bit worried about him, so went looking for him.

Later that night, when we were back to the gaff (place we were staying), I realised that because I had been snoring all the time the cheeky twats had given me my own room; my mate said that the racket I was making sounded like a train was flying past every few minutes, he said that the whole fackin' room was shaking. Anyway, due to the fact that we had been busy all day, I was knackered, so I'd take myself off to bed at seven every night. You see at the time I hadn't realised that my fatigue was due to the two heart attacks I'd had in the past, which, years later, I would find out about. Back then I didn't think of anything physical being wrong with me, I just put it down to the bumps I'd taken while sparring big heavyweights in the ring, people like Matt Legg and many other bruisers.

I would also go to bed really early when the boys were going into town for a booze-up. I was really tired all the time and felt like I'd been hit in the chest with a cannonball. This feeling reminded me of the slapping to my leg from my dad when I was in the ring; every time I went back to my corner, he would slap me on the leg, he'd slap me really hard and say: 'Dance boy, dance ... you need to dance son and keep out of his fackin' way!' This would always wind me up, but it worked, it made me stay out of my opponent's range and I'd out-box them and get a win. But back to the cannonball in my chest, this feeling went on for a few days, and I was so tired all the time. I kept telling myself it was the knocks, but it went on for fackin' years.

'Ere I'll tell you something I remember. Mind you, I'll have to be a bit careful how I put it across, but anyway, here goes...

There was this gigantic geezer in one of the clubs I was minding over in Bow; he was fackin' huge, he looked like something out of an old monster film. He was the biggest geezer I'd ever seen in my fackin' life; he was about six-foot eight and of Caribbean origin – I do hope that description was polite and PC enough? Anyway, he's giving it some in the middle of this club – he must've been on something, talking himself up with his, 'I'm this, I'm that, I'm Jackie-fackin'-Chan.' Yeah, 'course you are mate, I was thinking to myself, as he stood there dancing about doing martial arts moves with his hands all out in front of him. At one point with the way he was weaving his hands about right in front of my face I thought he was trying to send me into some sort of a fackin' trance!

Anyway, this was all getting a little out of hand, I was looking over at my brother Alfie, waiting for him to give me the nod to make a move, while my pal Kevin Wilson was all the time stood at the back of the big geezer, with bottle in hand, waiting for any sign of him kicking off, at which point Kev would go into action. Mind you, the man was about two feet taller than Kev, so he'd have had to jump on a table in order to plant the fucker on his bonce – fuck me, I thought to myself, somethings gotta give in a minute, otherwise I'm gonna steam in. Then he starts going on about it being his fackin' turf and I'm thinking: what is this, *The Warriors* or something? 'Cos he's informing us that he runs some club up the road up West, called Browns.

At this point, I'd seen enough, so I steamed over to him shouting, growling and bawling in his face. I put my hands on him, just to let him feel my strength and power! This knocked him back a bit, he could see I meant business, and all the while I was hollering up into his smug face: 'Do you want some, you ugly looking mug? 'Cos I'll rip your throat out for ya … I'll have it with all of you, you bunch of fackin' wannabe nobodies! Come on, let's have it … let's have ya!' I'm shouting as I'm shunting him and his entourage outside to the car park, then suddenly, it was over, they've just walked off, and I thought, thank fuck for that, 'cos I bet I'd have had my work cut out with that lot.

You see that's how these things can go. Because sometimes a little dispute like that would often turn into an all-out war, and then another time, such as with this incident, the troublemakers retreat and take their party on somewhere else. And the throwing down of their arms is all down to a little bit of bravado on my part; a battle won by my good self before it starts, aided by my ruthless and unflappable bit of confidence. Fackin' worked though, didn't it?

I was working at this place called Directors over in Milton Keynes for Richard Graham. It was a right rough old place, all the local hard-nuts and villains went in there: these were tough guys from the local estate as well as bouncers from other venues who were looking for a row to bolster their heightening reputation around the manor. And Richard, knowing how I am, put me in there to calm the place down. And on this particular night they were definitely all in there: the brawlers, the scrappers, the wannabe gangster gatecrashers; and they were all boozed up and looking for trouble. This place was to your average bouncer a fackin' nightmare, but to me it was like a lunatics' playground: a place where, if required, I might have to unleash the beast and let him go to work – but I never wanted that to happen! Deep down I always hoped for a quiet night: get in, get out, and get home to the wife. But, as it would seem, that's not what the locals wanted for me, and sometimes a debt would have to be paid. Not with money though – with my fists.

One particular night when all the local mental cases had turned up in droves, I could feel something building; hate was in the air and the Tequila slammers were flowing as this bunch of local fearsome lunatics started to play up. Now, these geezers are a handful on their own, and not many would fancy the job of tackling them one-on-one, never mind as a unit, but I'm 'Stormin' Norman' and don't give two shiny-shites about reputations, apart from my own, which I am totally and utterly comfortable with.

So, the voices are getting louder, the insults to the staff are mounting, and I'm stood there listening and watching, just waiting for this volcano to erupt. These scrappers and knifers need to be put in their place and it's my job to do it. Now, these boys were animals, so I knew I'd have to have my wits about me as I went over and ordered them to step outside the club. You see, this is a bit about bravado, 'cos immediately I go over, this bunch are obviously thinking, this cunt must be something if he's asking us lot outside, so already, hopefully, their guard is down a bit.

Seconds later we're outside the club, and I instantly turn it on, the beast is in full swing, and he's got the fackin' hump. So I'm stood there in a 'Rocky Marciano' style boxing stance offering the lot of 'em to step up into my space and have a straightener. (Marciano, the great American boxer, was the only heavyweight champion to finish his career undefeated.) These geezers looked a bit shaken; they're wondering what this lunatic has in his armament that is big enough and frightening enough to take them on when they're firm-handed. And thankfully, the confusion they were experiencing had all but won the battle for me, and

I'm continuously screaming obscenities at them to step up to the fackin' plate. Suddenly, and without a fist being released from its holster, it's over, 'cos not a soul among them wants to test me and they leave. They're looking slightly embarrassed, and, I imagine they're feeling a little less self-assured.

I had this geezer who was in training for the 21 SAS corps. He seemed like a nice enough sort of geezer and he was about six foot six inches in height and could have caused a bit of a row if needed. I wouldn't say he was an out-and-out brawler, but he could hold his hands up a bit. But the problem was that he was a bit of a spiteful cunt, and he started to get on my fackin' nerves. I remember he took this boy who had Down's Syndrome over to a local fairground and coaxed him onto the big wheel and taunted him and that – what an evil fucker. Anyway, I thought, I'll have you for doing that and I coaxed him onto the same big wheel with me.

Now, talk about The Mad Hatter, well, I was like him, but on an acid trip; I was a ravin' nutter. Anyway, I thought, you're having it you cunt, and when we got right to the very top, I made out I was yanking the safety bar out, I was shouting at the top of my lungs, going: 'Argh ... I'll open this shall I, son?' As I'm pushing and pulling this bar all over the place he was screaming, and I was roaring like an out-of-control gorilla. He was absolutely shitting himself, talk about the SAS, this geezer couldn't pass the training to mind for Mothercare! He was begging me to stop, but this just made me worse, and there I was almost yanking it out of its fackin' socket. He thought his time on this earth was over and I thought, GOOD ... that'll teach you not to frighten a young boy again.

To frighten him off for good, we planned something to scare him into an early grave. What happened was this. My brother, me and some mates used to go down to Hartwell church graveyard with masks on and jump out at the cars that were passing by, and in this way Chris Gallop and Vince Day would terrify the fackin' life out of geezers. So, one day, I said, bring this geezer who puts the frighteners on people over to the graveyard and we'll teach him a final lesson and get shot of him for good.

So, there was us lot all dressed up in white sheets down there, trying to look like ghosts. But we had a big fackin' cross and we had set it alight, so anybody who saw us would think we were the Ku Klux Klan; but in our naivety we just thought we looked spooky. Initially I had this old woman mask on and when I was crossing the road, Alfie was driving towards me with this geezer in the motor, with Alfie saying let's have her, but the geezer was shitting his pants, screaming and yelling: 'No – No – No … LET ME GO!' Remember, this is a s'posed SAS geezer, like. In the end Alfie let him go but said, we'll tell everyone that you were terrified. But he said, yeah but you haven't got any witnesses, and only us two know. He always said that when he'd been taken for a mug.

Anyway, this piss-taking geezer fucked off home, and our plan to get rid of him had hopefully done the trick. So, because we were all revved up, we drove into town to pick up some other geezers as they left the pub. The plan was to say we had a problem and needed them to help us and when we got 'em in the motors we would whiz off back to the graveyard and scare the shit out of them. Listen, it was Halloween … we had to get our kicks somewhere.

So, we rolled up at the boozer and picked these geezers up. Now, you have to remember these were tough boys – not just anybody; these were boys who worked the doors with us. Mind you, we did pick up Barry Bennett and a couple of other black geezers as well, so, when we arrived back at the graveyard it probably looked like we were on some sort of racist fackin' witch hunt; with the white sheets, burning cross and pig blood all over the gaff, it probably looked like we were organising some kind of sacrifice and they were going to be the victims of it. I don't know where Barry's head was, he must have been boozed up or something. Barry should've realised it was a joke, 'cos half of our firm were of African origin and we hated racists. In fact we ran racism out of Aylesbury when we were still in fackin' nappies. But Barry and his pals did a runner! They ran so fackin' fast they beat us back to town on foot, and we were in our motors! Mind you, during my antics with the mask on in the middle of the road I did jump into a bush full of stinging nettles and was in agony for the rest of the evening.

8

RAVIN' LUNATIC

Writers' Note

A raving lunatic doesn't mean he's top dog! It isn't meant to suggest that he's unbeatable. It simply means that back in his heyday, this man never gave a thought for who he went up against; it suggests that he was nuts; a loose cannon; an individual who never weighed up the odds before going into battle. Although, in essence, it's a header that I hope speaks for itself.

I remember one afternoon; I was taking a nice little leisurely stroll around Aylesbury town centre with me boy Jay tucked up seven feet high on my shoulders. Unbeknown to Jay, this was my eyes and ears up there, and it acted like my very own ship's periscope that my boy was in control of. Because you see, high up above the crowds, Jay could spot trouble coming from a mile away! And that way, I could get myself ready for whatever was coming.

Suddenly, Jay was yanking on my jacket as this geezer came over saying, 'There's some travellers round the back who wanna' fight you.' So, anyway, I asked him to take me to them, and off I went, hot on his heels. My boy Jay never had a clue what was about to happen. I don't think he'd have been scared 'cos my kids are used to it; they're street savvy and know only too well what kinda' work I'm involved in.

When we got round the back of the shops there was this big ugly looking cunt and he's towering above me. Apparently this geezer had a good reputation and was also a lot younger than me; he was so tall he was staring at my boy (who was obviously still on my shoulders) straight in the eyes. With that I lifted my boy down from my shoulders and said to the geezer, 'Right ... you've got a minute to throw your best shots and knock me out, and I won't throw nuffin' back. Now, if you manage it, my son here will hand you my Tom (tomfoolery – jewelry) ... it's yours to keep as a trophy! But you gotta' knock me clean out though ... no half measures!'

So, with that I takes off my big gold chain, and hangs it around me boy's neck: 'There ya go, son,' I said. 'Look after your old dad's necklace while I sort this naughty mister out.' With hope in his eyes Jay watched me as I slipped the chain around his small neck and gave him a little reassuring wink to steady his nerves.

So I walked over to the big bruiser – and believe me he was a big fucker – not as well-built and bulky as I was, but he was a big bastard all the same. Anyway, he started to unload shots into me; he was giving it all he had and smashing a granny into me. If I'm honest the odd one he landed almost took the wind out of my sails, and the geezer working the clock must've been on Fergie time (meaning allowing lots of time for injuries, referencing football manager Alex Ferguson), 'cos that minute didn't half drag on a bit.

With that, someone called time and I'm still stood there as bold as brass without a mark on me. So, anyway I said to the geezer: 'Right, you've lost the chain son, and now it's my turn!' He didn't look very happy, 'cos up until that point, apart from looking a bit knackered, obviously he never had a mark on him either. To be honest, I felt a bit sorry for him, but hey, he never felt sorry for me while he was hard at it trying to destroy me, and BANG, I've hit him with a thundering right-hander, which must've put the wind up his bunch of supporters 'cos they've immediately run off, leaving their pal on his own to take a beating.

Within a few seconds he was beat, but just to send out a message, I hit him with an uppercut that took him clean off his feet and shot him up off his trotters (feet), landing him in some big fuckin' iron skip. But listen, I ain't a horrible cunt, 'cos I've grabbed him by the arm, pulled him from the scraps and filth of the bin, shook his hand and said, 'Fair go, son ... no hard feelings, eh?' As I turned, I looked down and winked at my boy, then I slipped him back on my shoulders and took him off for a well-earned bite to eat in his favourite burger restaurant for children.

I remember one day having to go in a bit strong at a house to collect some dough for a car...

We turned up at this house, and Dad, who was too fuckin' crazy for his own good, stormed up at the front door as we stood back a bit in case it came on top – which it fuckin' did! But first, Dad worded the geezer up at the door, only the geezer wasn't playing ball and said, 'So you fellas think you've got the muscle to take on an army, do you?' To which Dad foolishly replied, 'What fuckin' army?' This was a big mistake. However, fortunately for Dad, as the door swung open someone spotted an axe peeping its head around the back door and shouted, 'Watch out Alf, he's got a fuckin' tool!' And as luck would have it, Dad had backed away from the door, just enough to get out of the way of this cunt planting what turned out to be an axe, in his fackin' head. Then suddenly, all hell broke loose!

Anyway, our lot have jumped out from behind the bushes: I say our lot 'cos we weren't fackin' stupid, we always planned these things a bit heavy just in case they come at us in numbers. I mean, I'm a ravin' lunatic and will fight an army, as will my dad and my brother, but if these geezers are tooled up and out for murder, six geezers from Aylesbury with their brains in the khazi (toilet) ain't walking out of there alive.

So, we've smashed the lot of them to pieces and there were bodies all over the place. But, as the odd one is coming round and popping their heads up trying to get a breather, one of our boys has stuck the boot into them and I'm shouting, 'Listen soppy bollocks, we need fackin' info (information) don't we?' 'Yes!' he hollered back. 'So,' I growled back at him, 'how the fuck are these cunts gonna sing (tell the truth) when you've put 'em back to fackin' sleep?' Anyway, with that he stopped giving it to 'em, and the ones we needed the intel from livened themselves up and squawked like a parrot in a pitbull's trap (mouth).

When you live the kind of life I do, even a normal day can turn into a moody one, and trouble's never too far away, 'cos there's always some wannabe fighter lurking round the corner waiting to get leery. One particular day springs to mind when I was just leaving the gym...

The thing is, having just done a bit of bag work and that, I was a bit pumped up already. So, I left the gym, jumped in the motor and I'm on my way home for a nice bit of a relax with the family. Then, as I came round this corner, some hooligans in a clapped-out bit of metal with more noise coming out their two-bit stereo than you get at a Who concert, almost took me off the fackin' road. They were cutting me up, then kept slowing down for me to overtake them and we had a bit of a chase going on. As I'd gone to overtake them, they immediately put their foot on their accelerator and sped up and nearly fackin' killed me. Well, that was it for me, and I was screaming and hollering out my window at 'em like a fackin' lunatic; the funny thing is these no-marks are screaming back at me as well, so, with that, I sped off down the road. At this point these boys must've thought they'd had a result; they must've thought my arse had gone twitchy and I'd had it away on my toes, full of fear. Well, how wrong can ya be, I remember thinking to myself, as I wheel-spun off down the road with these boys hot on my tail. What they didn't know was I was looking for somewhere to park up out of the way where there would be no eyes watching for evidence. And, just a few minutes later, I had found it; it was out of the way, down a little country lane, right off the beaten track. So, I pulled up and jumped out of my motor, ready for what was coming, and believe me, I was not at all fackin' happy.

Within no time, they screeched up beside me, and the four of 'em jumped out of their motor; tooled up and all aggressive, ready for a row. With that, they came at me: well three of them did, one of them stood back a bit and watched as I took his pals to pieces. To be honest, I was able to make light work of it 'cos as soon as I hit the first one and he flew across the grass, the other two geezers' arses went, they've half bottled it, so I just gave 'em a bit of a dig for coming after me. At which point I saw red, and I swear to God I went fucking mental. Now until you meet me and talk directly to me while looking me in the eyes, you really don't know what type of man I am, or the man I used to be. So, to give you a bit of information, back in those days I was a right fucking bastard – I didn't give a fuck for nobody – and those ingredients mixed up together made me one carefree opponent.

By this time, their other pal had jumped in the back seat of their motor, locked the doors and ducked his head down a bit so I couldn't see him. This was a shit plan on his behalf 'cos I spotted him immediately and started smashing the motor up. To be honest, this bit was all just bravado, I was simply putting the fear of God into him, and it did the trick instantly, so I fucked off home for a nice cuppa with the missus.

Later on that night, two policewomen arrived at my door, and when I answered it, more policemen jumped out of the bushes and quickly arrested me – I couldn't believe it. But that was that, they carted me off to the police station. Oh, I had also kept my attackers' iron bar and the knife, so I handed those over to them as evidence. I remember saying to them, 'Listen, mate, those boys attacked me first ... I'm innocent.' Now, I must have blacked out during the tear-up, 'cos the Old Bill went on to tell me that I had apparently smashed up their car with the iron bar as well.

About a year or so later a good friend of mine Matt Legg (a boxer, and a bloody good contender), told one of these boys to pick me up; apparently the geezer who hid in the back seat of that motor before was a pal of Matt's and Matt was on a bit of a wind-up and had rung me earlier to be in on it. So, as I was stood about waiting, this motor pulled up and I hopped in the back and said to Matt's pal, 'Hello, son ... don't I know you from somewhere?' Well, this poor geezer took one look in his driver's mirror, coughed, spluttered and went as white as a fackin' sheet. But before I'd had time to wind him up some more Matt's burst out laughing and blurted out, 'Fu...ck...in' 'ell Steve, I thought you was gonna dive out the motor and do a runner!' Anyway, it turned out this Steve was a really nice fella, and we laughed about it for ages after. Matt was boxing later that night in Watford I think it was, or perhaps Luton; they put a good traveller up against him, but Matt bashed him all over the place.

Talking about travellers, I always got on well with them and I trained a good many of them as well. One particular traveller's dad said to me recently, that if his son hadn't gone over to America, I could have made him a champion. I used to spar with a load of up-and-coming boxers, and I toughened them right up in the process. Travellers can be tough old boys, and if you nurture them properly, they'll be loyal and stick with you right to the bitter end.

People used to turn up and train with me at all hours. They would even show up at two in the morning as well. People from all walks of life would be there, from local travellers that I knew, to people I had never even seen before. At times people say to me, how many bouts have you had, and I honestly haven't got a fackin' clue: to me it's like asking how many cups of tea I've had ... I wouldn't even like to guess.

The rave scene had just kicked off and they were happening all over the country. Tony Hayter was 'old school' and went about planning his raves by having a face-to-face sit-down with some carefully hand-picked farmer who had a lot of land with a big barn. Tony would hire the place for the night and put an event on; it was a right tasty little earner, and Tony knew just how to play it.

On the night of the show when the Old Bill turned up (which was a regular occurrence) Tony would just come up with a moody name for himself and make out he was the hired help – it was a load of bollocks, of course. But eh, Tony was as sharp as a butcher's blade; he knew exactly how to handle these kinds of people, and what is more, his scheming always fackin' worked.

I was working in one place where they had just finished filming the Hollywood blockbuster *Full Metal Jacket* and because they had only recently finished filming, they hadn't taken all the set away. Anyway, once again, the Old Bill turned up, but because there were loads of people there, they very quickly realised that they were totally outnumbered and wouldn't, or perhaps more realistically couldn't, make a move. Anyway, I wasn't interested in all the political red-tape crap, so I just made myself busy looking around the place at the bits that had been blown up while filming. I was intrigued walking around looking at all the scenery that had been left behind, like the coconut and palm trees and that. There was sand every-fackin'-where. Mind you, I bet the farmers didn't care, 'cos I imagine they made a fackin' killing back in the 1980s from all of those film companies.

Like I've mentioned previously, Tony was a right clever fucker: this geezer had security in every fackin' town you could think of, and could muster up an army of burly geezers for any place he was organising a rave in. So, there would be two hundred minders, bouncers and security blokes working the nights and not a soul could do a fackin' thing about it ... not even the police. Alfie, my brother, ran all the security. Alfie was a born organiser, he was very regimental, and had everything worked out for each man and the position they had to be in at any given venue. Our team was a finely tuned operation, and we even had dogs on the payroll as well.

While working these dos, I got to know some of those in the other rave lot. There was one rave organisation called Helter-Skelter, which was sited at an old airbase. Anyway, I got speaking to the farmer one day while some youngsters were messing about around us. Anyway, I said to the farmer, 'These lot are okay, mate … they're harmless enough, really.' When suddenly he started screaming and shouting, saying, 'Aargh, what are you doing!' This was because apparently some fackin' nutter who was pissing around had come up behind him and put his finger straight up his arse. Immediately, the raver apologised, saying, 'Sorry, I thought it was Norman!' Well, I was laughing so much I didn't know where to fackin' look. A little while later another raver came up to me, he was off his tits and said, 'Have you seen Norman?' To which I skittishly replied, 'Are you taking the piss or something, mate? I am fackin' Norman!' And he responded with, 'Oh, okay, sorry, I'll go and look for him then!' I just stood there laughing to myself; the geezer was on another fackin' planet.

Once, we went to a rave over in Hemel Hempstead. We had the dogs with us, and one of them was a big scary Rottweiler. Anyway, working with us was this big bloke called Bangers from Buckingham. So, we're all going about our usual regime when Bangers came over with his shirt all ripped to pieces, and I said, 'What's up with you, mate? What's fackin' happened to ya' shirt?' While he was holding a lead with no dog attached, he replied, 'I was holding the dog and it's gone and attacked me!' If I'm honest, what with all the drugs that were floating around, I wouldn't be surprised if most of the dogs were off their tits as well as the ravers.

This other time, we were on our way to a rave on New Year's Eve. There were about fifteen of us with a handful of snarling dogs, heading down the coast to this party. Anyway, as we approached, we noticed the Old Bill were waiting for us down at this bridge. I have to be honest, I thought it was Jeremy fackin' Beadle and his crew filming an episode of *You've Been Framed* or something; I honestly thought they were there in wait to jump out and do a number on us. But I was wrong, it really was the Old Bill, and they had a right poxy attitude with us. So, one of 'em piped up and said, 'If your dogs get a bit aggro, we'll fackin' shoot them!' I remember thinking, what a horrible cunt. After all it ain't the dog's fackin' fault, so why would this nasty cunt take it out on them? Thankfully, nothing like that happened, but after a bit of a disagreement they ended up locking us all up for the night, so that the rave couldn't go ahead.

We travelled all over the UK for the rave scene. We covered Birmingham, Wales, Scotland, London and it was going great. However, as is usually the case with stuff like this, things started getting a little bit naughty: people were getting shot and killed all over the place, and let's face it, it doesn't matter who the fuck you are, you ain't going toe-to-toe with someone who's pointing a sawn-off shotgun in ya' mush ... now are you? Well, that was that, my mind was made up and I thought, 'Now, what do you do if you wanna scare some silly cunt who's holding a shooter? I'll tell you what you do, Norm, you get a bigger fackin' shooter, and then see who wants to stick around to play cowboys and indians!' Listen, where I come from it's a no-brainer. So, that's what I did, I got myself a nice hefty twelve-bore sawn-off, and it worked as a new deterrent when my fists and head got relegated.

Another ex-squaddie pal of mine was a geezer called Colin Roberts...

Colin ran a gym called Reps in the Agora Shopping Centre. He was a big geezer and very capable and was another of the firm of boys who worked for Tony Ash and Charlie Beer. I was in the nick (prison) at the time when Col was running things for Tony Ash, but he told me that when I came out (after hearing all these stories about me) he said he saw me wandering around the Agora and asked someone who I was, and was told a bit lively, 'Oh that's Norman ... Stormin' Norman Buckland.' And he said he couldn't believe his eyes, and thought to himself, 'What? That's the legendary geezer I've heard so much about? The lunatic and big tasty fucker Stormin' Norman? And he's in here; in a shopping centre, acting as a static guard?' He said he thought, you're having a fackin' laugh, aren't you? But obviously he was right, 'cos that's exactly what I was doing.

A few weeks later I walked into Reps Gym and asked what they had to offer. With that Col handed me the pamphlet upside down and I pretended to read it, but I was having trouble doing so 'cos of my dyslexia; Colin didn't know this at the time, so when we started chatting about this and that and he happened to mention being posted out in the sunny climes of Spain, I jumped into a bit of the old Spanish lingo. Well, fuck me, he almost dropped to the floor! I could see his nut going, 'Eh? This geezer can't read a brochure in good old English, but he can reel off the Spanish lingo like one of the fackin' locals!' Col and I hit it off straight away, and I thought, we'll do a bit of work together one day. One such day arrived, and I asked him, 'Col, do you have half an hour to spare later, my old mate?' Anyway, he immediately said he was available, and the rest as they say...

So, my property dealer and I drove over to pick him up and told him that we had had some Kenyan geezers hauled up in one of my gaffs (properties) and my property geezer and I want 'em out. Moments later, we arrived at one of my properties, head up to the kitchen and there's this big fackin' lump stood there with the hump; this geezer obviously thinks he's in the right to be letting his pals stay gratis and without my consent and he's started to get a bit mouthy. With that he's ramped the agg up a gear and Col's belted him clean on the jaw and he's keeled over like a fackin' oak tree. So, I ran over to the sink, got a cupful of water, slung it in his face and said, 'Oi … wake-up, you cheeky cunt!' Col couldn't believe what he was seeing and he's laughing like a hyena on an acid trip. And I said to him, 'Col, you young cunt … I didn't want anyone to get bashed up!' We fucked off down the stairs and left this lot to pack up their clobber and have it away on their toes. All sorted, on to the next fackin' one.

A few weeks later, I received a call from Col's governor, Charlie Beer, to go down the Victoria in Wolverton 'cos his man down there was having a hard time with a handful of travellers. So, I shot down there to see what the score was. But on the way down I came across a pigeon with a busted wing, so I looked in the car boot, found an old shoe box, stuck the pigeon in it and got myself into the boozer.

When I walked in, I spotted that it was good old Col, and noticed this rowdy group of geezers to the left of him. Now, as Col said himself, he could've handled two or three of them on his jack, but he looked happy as fuck when I walked in, pleased I guess that I was there to back him up, and to even up the odds, which meant he didn't have to have a roll around single handed with five or six of them.

Anyway, he asked me what was in the box, and I told him. Well, he almost fell about laughing. I could see his point: he's ready to have a tear-up and I've strolled in to ease things with a broken bird in tow! Col told me that these geezers were looking for agg and I told him not to worry. I called these geezers over and told them if they fucked off in twenty minutes, next time they came in I'd buy 'em all a drink, but if they wanted to carry on with the aggravation, they could take their chances, and see what happened. And with that, they had a laugh and a joke and fucked off without a murmur. As a young geezer, I think Col learned a good thing that evening, about how to talk to people.

Mind you, I almost got into a bit of trouble one night down WKD Café in Camden Town when that 'Return of the Mack' geezer (the singer, Mark Morrison) tried coming it on the door, when his minder got a bit leery, so I bashed him and put him to sleep where he stood. Apparently, this Mark geezer was down there to do a promotional PA and I've banged his bodyguard out cold. Col told me later that he'd received a call from his governor, ranting down the blower saying, your man Norman has only gone and sparked out the celebrity's fucking minder. But Col told me he said to his governor, 'Listen, he must've been a right horrible cunt, 'cos Norman's a nice geezer and wouldn't give him a seeing-to for no reason.' Anyway, I think I got away with that one – no harm done. Well, apart from the harm I done to the chippy fackin' minder who had too much to say for himself!

9

THE BUCKLAND BROTHERS

Writers' Note

'So ya wanna be a boxer, in the golden ring.' Well, these brothers did, and following in the footsteps of their fist-fighting forefathers was what it was all about; it was on the cards, and that twenty by sixteen-foot roped off bit of canvas, was soon to become their playground.

Brothers, right where do I begin? Okay, so, at least nine out of ten of born and bred Buckland family men always end up doing a bit of boxing: it's just part of our heritage; it's simply what we were born into. And if, as a young boy coming up, you display something a little special, then all the Buckland men get right behind you. And that right there is just how it all started for me and my brother Alfie. Alfie had the most technical promise, while I had more heart than a lioness protecting her fackin' babies.

You see, when you live like us, when you walk down the stairs in the morning and see all your dad's trophies out on display, it gives you that little bit of an edge, and you look at 'em all shiny and appealing and think, 'I'll have a piece of that.' Moreover, when you go to school and the other kids show you newspaper clippings of your dad who had boxed some geezer from Luton the night before, and won, you go, oh yeah, that's my dad and feel proud. And it's stuff like that that makes you want to enter into the game yourself.

There was boxing on both my mum and my dad's sides of the family, so that meant that images of boxing were always around us. My aunty married a pro boxer called Billy DC, who ended up boxing the likes of the Finnegan brothers etc. And again, the kids at school would ask, 'Was that your uncle fighting on *Grandstand* last night?' And Alfie and I would be as proud as punch knowing that everybody knew these geezers were fighters, and even better, that they were geezers from our family.

It was Aylesbury Boxing Club where it all began, which later moved to Quarrendon School. At the time it was run by a couple of geezers called Vic and Pete. It wasn't heavy at that time, because we were only young: just a bit of skipping and bag work to get us used to being around a boxing gym environment. But this was a well-established place, fighters like Oscar Angus came out of there, and he was the uncle of Richard Graham, who was a very good friend of ours. This club was proper blood, sweat and tears; a real down and dirty affair with the coaches walking around with fags hanging from their lips as they shouted and hollered instructions. It was a good eye opener for me and my brother; it was a place where you would very quickly come to the realisation as to whether the sport was for you or not.

My dad then started a new club called Meadowcroft Boxing Club. And due to my dad's name, it became established very quickly, with a lot of the top boys from around the area going there. It was only a little scout hut, but we had all the facilities over there, with a proper ring, bags, pads, the lot

– everything you needed for a good old-fashioned boxing gym. And having all the top geezers from around the area attending meant I quickly picked stuff up, and learnt how to throw a proper right-hander, from an extremely young age. And this, which you will very quickly realise as you read on, became a very useful attribute to have when faced with what was to come in my life.

Alfie and I were each a right fackin' handful separately, but as brothers going into any sort of battle, well fackin' hell you would have had to throw in the towel if you were up against us. 'Cos, we didn't give a fuck! We knew what we was capable of, and for the most part, so did every fucker on our manor. From Bucks to Kentish Town, our names were feared, revered, and noted as being intimidating. From town to town we were talked about with admiration; not as bullies, but as respected men who always got the job done. Listen, we were the new kids on the block, and nothing and nobody was ever going to get in our way. Oh, and in the early days, we had another bullet locked and loaded in our gun: our old fella, or Dad if you haven't already worked it out. Listen, our dad was the archetypal force to be reckoned with: resolute, durable, and intensely persuasive. Dad had a clear set of unique ways of dealing with people and fuck me, was he immovable! When Dad belted you on the chin, you had just a few seconds to answer with a resounding apology, in expectation of his acceptance of your penitence. And that would be the only thing left between a troublemaker and a trip down-town with the paramedics.

But back to the Buckland brothers ... now what can I say? Well, from the day we nicked each other's dummies, to the day we pick up our divvies, Alfie and I will always be there for one another. Oh, we fight each other ... fackin' hell, do we fight one another! Yeah, but listen, at times I do his fackin' nut in; it's just my way ... I can't help it. Look, I've had that many knocks to my head, it's damaged the inner workings of my brain a bit, and for that reason alone at times I can be a fackin' nightmare – I can be hard work. I'm a fackin' nuisance, and I spit my dummy out of me pram when my brainbox goes all out of tune. I don't mean any harm, I'm just like a grumpy little kid in a grizzly bear suit. And a pairing like that is difficult to control. ''Ere, who said that? Who said I was fackin' paranoid?'

I think it goes back to being a young boy. I think it echoes back to a time when I felt ridiculed and misunderstood. But as a boy I just got on with it and accepted it as my lot! However, I honestly believe that when I got older and saw my pals getting on in life, it hit me hard and played havoc with me psychologically. And from that day forward I think I attacked myself for not doing better with my education. I pulled myself down for not trying harder at school. But my theory is: if someone you look up to as your superior tells you enough times that you're illiterate and thick, then very quickly you will start to believe it. And over time, it becomes a part of your fackin' make-up. So, as my writer pal says: 'Listen, Norm, don't blame yourself ... blame the bloody system!' And for the sake of my sanity, I think I'll do just that. Anyway, it makes me feel better not thinking it was solely down to me.

'Ere you sent me off track then ... right where was I? Oh yeah, The Buckland Brothers ... So, like I said, from Bucks to Timbuktu every fucker and his bulldog knew about us. Our names spread through the streets like street sellers on poppy day. But unfortunately, along with that came the wannabe gangsters who wanted to prove themselves.

I remember Alfie had a bit of a barny with a fellow boxer called Randy something. He had really rubbed my brother up the wrong way and the dishing out of a few spankings was inevitable. We ended up chasing these cunts over to the local hospital, which was perfect for me and our Alfie, 'cos after they'd been ironed out, they wouldn't have far to crawl. But on this occasion, it wasn't to be! 'Cos as soon as we caught up with them, this Randy geezer got down on his hands and knees and was begging for mercy. I offered his pals up for a tear-up, but all to no takers, and it was over. We left them there squirming and looking totally embarrassed.

To be honest, back in the day, it was never really about me and my brother fighting shoulder-to-shoulder; it was more about being safe in the knowledge that we were there for each other. When we were young we once got in a row at home, and just like brothers we went at it, brawling, and Alfie was getting the better of me. Now, my brother and I were as stubborn as each other, and on any given day you could flick a coin to decide the winner. I've always been your typical British Bulldog, but Alfie was clever and more methodical, and while I hammered into him, he would wait patiently and then start cherry-picking shots off to finish me. Dad, forever the scrapper, was egging us on: but Mum watched on in disgust. Dad's idea was to leave us to fight and get it out of our systems. While Mum's attitude was more to point out to us that fighting brought no good outcomes for anyone.

However, on this occasion our Dobermann dog stuck his two-bob's worth in, as he sunk his devastating fangs into Alfie's mouth, ripping his lip apart. Claret was gushing, and Alfie was raging as he chased me off into the bathroom. Outside, Alfie was trying to appeal to my innocence, saying:

'C'mon Norm … let's forget all about it, no harm done, eh?' But on this occasion I was boxing clever, I wasn't taking any fackin' notice, I knew he'd lost his head and was ready to iron me out proper. So, I slipped out through the window and left him to calm the fuck down. Hours later, after a few stitches and a telling-off from our mum, Alfie and I were back to being brothers again.

Our dad was only five feet four inches tall, but if you saw his hands before you saw him, you'd think he was a giant, 'cos they were fackin' huge! He had hands like a fackin' cave troll, just like Grandad Bucky and Gypsy Jack Cooper. These fellas' hands were so big that they would need to have their rings specially made. Dad was a proper power-house, and without much strain at all he could pick a big geezer up with one hand and launch him straight across a street. So, like I said earlier when he belted me, and I never felt a thing, he thought I was from another planet; he couldn't believe how much pain I could take.

Much like my dad, Alfie always put me on the right path. I mean, even the experience that I just mentioned proved to be a learning tool for me. It taught me to always be on my guard and ready for anything; it taught me that instead of going at it hell-for-leather and knackering myself out, I should do as he did and bide my time until the right opportunity came to unleash the proper shots at the desired moment. And in my mid to late teens during my boxing bouts this helped me no end. Alfie was always calm and systematic and knew exactly when to be methodical and when to turn it on and be a bit more brutal. And this worthy piece of free education I applied to my own style of fighting. Alfie had inadvertently taught me a whole new box of tricks, and I adapted my way of fighting to accommodate this.

I mean, he was never going to turn me into Alfie mark three, but I knew that I could use the tools he'd shown me cleverly. Listen, I'll always be a lunatic … that will never change, but a little bit of holding back went a long, long way. And when I minded the door, I would only unleash the inner beast if, and I do mean, IF, it was absolutely necessary. And if I'm honest, I would say that for at least 70 per cent of my time spent looking after clubs and boozers it never was necessary. On most occasions I could calm an assailant down by simply talking to him; I'd have a word in his ear, he'd see reason and very quickly start to relax. And sometimes, I'd even pay for a taxi home for them and send them on their merry way: it was anything to get the job done. Furthermore, I would treat every case on its merits.

I remember while working WKD in Kentish Town throwing ice at the other bouncers. I would stand right at the top balcony, out of the way, and hurl big lumps of ice at one of them stood down below. It was hilarious watching him blame the other bouncer; he'd be ranting and raving like a fackin' lunatic, asking the other geezer why he'd thrown ice at him. And I'd be watching and giggling like a two-year-old on Smarties. Well, who wants to be a moody cunt all the time? The job was boring and shit at times, and fackin' around made the hours tick by.

I got asked to work in the rectory farm with a pal of mine, Leroy Dennis; Leroy was a top-class minder. He'd had a bit of trouble with some brothers who had smashed him up with iron bars, and they ended up doing a few years' poky for it. Anyway, he rang me up saying his mother was having some trouble off the same people up town and it was putting the wind up her, so I said I'd have a word. Now my brother had had a run in with them a few years earlier and he'd smashed them both up, but this geezer was a bit strange: I don't know what it was but he always had a problem with doormen. So, I said to him, 'Look, if you keep fucking about in the clubs I'm working at, I won't just give you a slap anymore, I will fackin' shoot you.' He knew I wasn't one to make idle threats.

So, anyway, one night when I was full of aggro and wanted a little retribution, I went round his house and kicked his fackin' door down. Then, all of a sudden, he appeared from nowhere, and, lo and behold, to my astonishment, he was wearing a ladies pink nighty with a face full of fackin' make up: big bright red lipstick, the fackin' lot. I couldn't believe what I was seeing and thought to myself, this cunt's gotta fackin' go! So, there I was stood right in front of the geezer (well sort of) aiming a twelve-bore shotgun straight at him, when suddenly, he's shat himself where he was standing and fainted. The stench was horrible, and I had to get away, so I shot out a few of his windows and fired at some potted plants, shot a few barrels into his motor and had it away on my toes. Well, I had to, 'cos I'd have looked a right cunt when Plod (the coppers) turned up and found me with my tool in my hand standing over Quentin Crisp!

Later that evening I arrived home to find the Old Bill there in force waiting for me; I went quietly 'cos I knew I'd been rumbled; fuck knows how many people must've witnessed it. I was absolutely loopy towards the end, everything had caught up with me, the raves, the door work, steroids, the lot, my head was totally fucked up and the stress and overpowering depression was hitting me hard – sometimes I'd stand at the bus stop and when a bus was flying towards me, I'd think about ending it all by jumping in front of it! So, as I'm sure you'll agree, at that time I really needed to get my head in gear. Would prison prove to be the best place for me? Well, let's see…

10

THE BIRDMAN O' WOODHILL

Writers' Note
Some go to prison for an education in criminality. Some go because it's simply a by-product of their chosen career. Some even go for a holiday. However, our protagonist was somewhat different, for this man went to get back his life; this man went for the sake of his sanity!

So, it's finally come on top! But to be honest I wasn't bothered, I deserved it, I mean, who picks up a shooter and marches round to some geezer's house and goes to town on his stone cladding, while pepper spraying his plant pots with lead and thinks they're gonna tootle off back to life whistling a happy tune? Well not me, it was obvious, everybody knows me, and every dog and its owner knew I had a beef (problem) with this fella: his mouth was as wide as the fackin' Mersey; he'd been badgering me for years, I'd had more little rumbles with this man than I'd had hot dinners, he was a fackin' nightmare. Anyway, in the end after many warnings, I smashed into him and threw him through a window; he got the hump about that and started threatening me with a shooter. Then, one day I heard he was after my family and that tipped the balance. So that's when I went round to his

147

house and acted out my version of the Mafia's Valentine's Day massacre. Stupid thing to do, but I was a fackin' loose cannon – I didn't give a fuck for no one.

To cut a long story short I ended up at the Old Bailey getting ten years; I received a five stretch for the firearms and five for affray, but fortunately, I only ended up doing three for the affray bit.

So, for that little bit of naughtiness, I got life'd-off! Well okay, not exactly life'd-off, but seven fackin' years. 'Ere don't laugh, 'cos seven years away from my family truly was like a fackin' lifetime to me! I didn't think I'd handle it, I thought I'd go absolutely fackin' loopy; I imagined myself ending up in Broadmoor chasing invisible butterflies around with a teacup in an empty cell. Anyway, there was no way out of it, listen, I didn't have the judge and his peers in my pocket. I was had, and on my way to do my bit of porridge, from the courthouse to the jailhouse with no stops for tea and tiffin on the way.

Prison wasn't really a deterrent for me. 'Cos like I've stated, at that time in my life I didn't really give a fuck for nothing or nobody. This for me was just par for the course; in my line of work, it was inevitable that everyone at some time or another has to be prepared to do a bit of Stir, Nick, Bird, Jug, Choky, or whatever else you want to call it. You can even call it Porridge, as the title of the next bit informs you. I guess every area of the country has its own nickname for jail, and most prisoners from newbies to old lags will have their favourite moniker for it. Anyway, it was my turn to do a stint; it came just at the right time, and for all the right fackin' reasons. And in the security van on the way down, I remember thinking to myself, 'Right Guv ... let's fackin' do this!'

They knew I was on my way. This was obvious 'cos they were all there waiting for me as I arrived; they must've tooted it through on their prison fackin' whistles or something. It was nice though, and it made me feel like a king. The Françoise brothers were on '1A' (wing) waiting for me with a phone so that I could stay connected to my family. What a nice pair of geezers, taking the time to sort me out a bit of pay-as-you-go communication to my loved ones.

Woodhill had the typical layout. It was sparse, full of steps, landings and pool tables; it was bright and clinically white, enough to give your arse a headache. But they had beds, grub and a telly, so I thought to myself: Norman, this gaff is like home from home, so get your head down and sleep the months away.

As soon as I entered the main bit of the prison, the cons were out in force waiting for me to walk out onto the landing; even the screws welcomed me with open arms, it was weird. Look I know I'm The Guv'nor but as far as I was aware, they would only allow one governor in the nick (prison) and that's the one sat in his office dishing out orders. Fortunately, I was wrong, and during my time in Woodhill I became part of the furniture; they kept me there on remand for almost two years; to be quite truthful, I think they liked me being there as much as I fackin' did. It sounds stupid that doesn't it? But I'm telling you, I needed to be locked up for a while, to get my head in check, and to rewire my boss-eyed brain.

This place was like home from home, having said that it was even better, 'cos I probably had more respect in the jail than I did on the streets – and that's fackin' saying something: on the streets I was The Guv'nor but in there, I was the same, and then some, it was perfect. I used to walk up and down those landings, and everybody would be on their best behaviour. And if some young YP (young prisoner) was playing up and the screws were having a bit of agg (aggravation) with him, they'd send me in to growl at him and word the boy up. And if it just happened to be a little firm who were making a proper nuisance of themselves, I'd ramp it up a bit and do a little more growling, snarling, and believe me, they'd listen. Oh, and if I went in there a bit heavier, shouting and screaming telling 'em what I'd do if they didn't liven themselves up, even the screws would jump to attention.

I couldn't believe my eyes one day. I was walking along looking inside the sheds, day-dreaming away to myself, thinking how my life would be when I got released, when suddenly, from out of fackin' nowhere, who walks up to me? It was only my good pal Matt Legg. Anyway, I asked him what the fuck he was doing in Springhill, and he told me that him and Kevin Wilson, another great pal of mine, had both been sent there and that they were on C wing – I was gobsmacked, I couldn't believe what I was seeing. Matt had obviously been up to his old tricks and got himself a little stretch, but I'll get onto that a bit later, but I got to tell you this now while I remember. After Matt and Kevin had done their time and had been out a while I was walking one day when I heard, 'Hello Norm … how ya doing Guv?' I was gobsmacked as I stood there wondering what was going on, I thought I was going fackin' mad 'cos Matt had done his bird and had been released from nick a long while back. And I said, 'What the fuck are you doing here, son?' And he replied, 'I've got Kevin Wilson with me, Norm … we've broken in specially to see you!' Now, I've heard of breaking out of choky, but never the other fackin' way round! Anyway, it was so nice to see them both and we had a good old chat, but back to the story, fuck where was I? Ah yeah that's right.

The nonce wing was a horrible place, and every man and his dog hated the cunts that lived there. These animals were the worst people in the prison and according to most of the inmates (not to mention the odd screw – say no more) they needed to be taught a lesson. And if you got even the slightest chance to get to them, you'd give it to them. And I don't mean give them a bit of your canteen, I mean hurt 'em and let me tell you, they got it; sometimes you felt bad when you went a bit strong with them, but most of these horrible bastards had killed little ones, and the ones they hadn't done away with: the boys and girls they'd savagely raped and tormented, well their lives were all but ruined, the mental torture shit had got in their heads and they tortured themselves with it ever after. Some of these poor unfortunates even believed it was their own fault. So, it was just a fact of 'prison-inmate-protocol' that these worthless pieces of shit needed a dig and let me tell you this: they were swiftly dealt with.

I was with Matt Legg one day as I went to word one of these horrible cunts up. I wanted to show Matt what I was all about; teach him what was right and wrong in the world; show him when to go in all-guns blazing and when to relax a bit and just growl in their faces. Matt was a good boy, but he'd got in with the wrong lot and wound up going way over the top and landing himself in jail. Matt was better than that: he had talent as a boxer, and I was more than willing to share with him what I knew – and that's exactly what happened. Matt had a lot of ability, and when he hit you, believe me you knew you had been hit. However, his feet were all over the place; he lacked technical knowhow and I was the one to balance it out. Listen, this boy was used to all-in street fighting, no style, no grace, just good honest brawling, remember, this had been my game on the streets for a long while, so I knew all the angles; I knew the best way to deal with him, or perhaps even those that were in front of you.

Anyway, we turned up at this pervert's cell and I told Matt to hang back and take it in. So, I walked in the door and surprised the pervert with a deafening roar: 'Right, listen here you fackin' horrible bastard,' I hollered at him, almost spitting in his face. 'Listen, if I see you look at any of the boys on the wing funny ... if you so much as look in the direction of one of the YPs ... I'm gonna come back here and do you. And when I say do you, I mean finalise you ... over ... brown bread, you hearing me? You horrible waste of a carcass?' The nonce didn't even open his eyes: he just put his head in his hands and screamed: 'I'm sorry ... I'm sorry ... I promise I won't ... I promise!' I turned to Matt, winked, and walked from the cell. 'See that cunt, son ... he won't dare leave his cell for a few days ... RESULT!' 'Fackin' hell Norm,' Matt said, 'I think I'll stay in my cell, too!' And the two of us laughed all the way back to the wing. Lesson over. A growl is sometimes better than a dig, 'cos the fear and apprehension of what is to come is sometimes far more frightening than what actually happens.

Matt was a fantastic pupil, if that's what ya wanna' call him. He was a great listener for his age, which, for an up-and-coming boxer is one hell of an essential characteristic. So we could train properly, I tried to get gloves and pads in the nick, but it was a no-go, because the governor was having none of it. Apparently, he said, 'If you let this man ... Storming ... erm ... whatever his name is, train all the YPs to box, it's simply rabble-rousing; these people might try and take over my own prison ... and that would be disastrous

'Ere, I told you I didn't always look like a bulldog': Alfie and me as pageboys at
Auntie Moira's wedding. Moira married Uncle Billy DC,
a professional boxer.

Globetrotting in Xávea with L-R: Aunty Josie, Mum, Alfie, Gran and me.

Yours truly, gloved-up, with Dad (the pad man) and Alfie
(the cooler-king) at Aylesbury Gym, Dad's boxing club.

On the sofa at home, Cassie (my first born)
likes to dress me up. Well, that's my excuse
and I'm sticking to it!

My first house in Wolverton.
I'm just a pup of 24 years old in
this photo.

Down Great Yarmouth with Brandon,
Jay and Cassie.

Here in my big gaff next to my bungalow where we live now. With my son, Jay.

On the sofa in the big house, 35 years old. Eh, check out the tough geezer behind me.

Xávea, Spain, 38 years old. L-R: Eric Houston, Matt Legg, Richard Graham and me.

Outside Aylesbury Registry Office. L-R: Cowboy, Barry Bennett,
James Buckland and Stevan Wilson.

In Spain with my dad, 38 years old.

L-R: Me, Kevin Wilson, Alfie (brother),
Dave Courtney and Big How at Dave's
party up north.

In Benidorm to sort some trouble out with Frankie Ross.

I love animals, especially dogs – these are two of mine, Bullseye and Storm.

The Guv'nor's gym (down the barn). L-R: Gavin (friend), Issa (grandson), Eric Houston (my BFF), Jay, Jamaal (grandson), Norman, Ray 'Uncle 'Arry Carter (godfather) and Nassir (son-in-law).

In Xávea (my second home), Spain with Alfie, my youngest boy.

My comeback, at 47 years old. This fight was held at Caesar's Palace with Dick James in my corner (just after this photo was taken, I jumped out of the ring and knocked out some geezer who was playing-up).

My son, Brandon, at one of his fights at Caesar's Palace. L-R: Me, Brandon and Tracey (my first wife).

Still a hard bastard at 45 years old.

Right, who's brave enough to get down the barn?

Me and Nanette on our wedding day in the Philippines. 'Love her to pieces'.

Good ol' Charlie Bronson peering over my shoulder.
Some newspaper tried to stir-up a bit o' beef between us!

L-R: James, who's the Guv'nor, Manny Clark and his mates, in some London boozer.

… damned stupidity,' he said. 'No, I like how this man has got the boys in order on the landings, but there could be a bloody mutiny if we let him and his merry men loose with boxing gloves.' So, that was the end of that! But our heads were working overtime, what else could we use instead?

Anyway, after weighing up the odds, we decided that the best thing to use were socks, yeah, fackin' socks; great itchy prison socks with big fackin' holes in them. Well, if that was the best we were gonna get, we were gonna have to make do. 'C'mon son,' I said to Matt, 'let's get over to the shower block and have a bit of a spar-up.' And that was exactly what we did!

It was perfect, we could move about in there as free as we liked: Matt, with a sock on each hand, doing the hitting, and me, tooled-up to the nines with three pairs of socks on me hands as his pad-man (the one who accepts the cushioned punches, as a way of teaching the novice). And as I took him on the pads, most of the wing would gather round from a distance and watch in awe as Matt went to work smashing a granny out o' me 'ands! I mean c'mon people, our work in that nick back then was bloody visionary! Well, we thought it was. Mind you, it probably looked fackin' mental to the officials: two big lumps with socks on their hands going at it hammer-and-tongs – fackin' priceless!

I remember while we were training in the gym one afternoon and one of the screws tried to come-it a bit. He wanted me to do two plates (the disc-shaped weights on the bar) a side on the weights bench for fifty reps (repetitions) at a time, he was just being a prick trying it on. My mate Buchannan was there at the time, and even he knew I wanted no part of it. Anyway, when I went to walk past him he pushed me back and stood in my way. Right, I thought, fuck it I'm not having that, so I gave him a few light body shots and he went down on the floor like a ton of bricks. He folded in half like a bit of paper: the wind was completely taken out of his sails, and he was coughing and spluttering like a two-bob car engine. I helped him up and said, 'Sorry, boss, but you went a bit too far … no harm done, eh?' But he wasn't happy, he swung out his battle stick and smashed it on the emergency button and an army of screws immediately came to his rescue. This was totally out of order because this cunt knew exactly what he was up to. I was pissed off and I said to them all, 'Listen, I was only playing with him … I didn't mean to knock him to the floor! Look, I only gave him a few slaps to the belly and he's on his arse.' But they weren't having any of it and took me back to the wing. I was punished for that little episode, as they banned anybody from my wing going down the gym for a bit.

On another occasion, my mate was giving them a bit of shit. I tried warning him to back off, but he took no notice and just continued. Now, this mate of mine was a bit of a Jack-the-lad, he had two girlfriends on the outside and would write to the two of them, separately, all the time. The screws bided their time with him and one day got their own back on him when they swapped the addresses round on the letters to his girlfriends, and obviously this meant that each of them would read what he was saying about the other woman. He wasn't at all happy, but I told him it was his own fault 'cos he was always fucking with these screws. I'd told him many times that they wouldn't put up with his bullshit, but he just wouldn't listen. It still makes me laugh, imagining those girls' faces as they opened their letters – I bet his name was shit around his manor for a while.

Aside from me trying to keep the young lads in line while I was doing my bit of bird, without even knowing it, I almost turned into Robert Stroud from that film *The Birdman of Alcatraz*. It wasn't a manufactured thing, it just fackin' happened. I mean, I've always been an animal lover, and I detest horrible bastards that hurt them, I really do. But my looking after and nurturing the animal world's waifs and strays in Woodhill prison just came out of nowhere. And it was the screws that gave me the title of Birdman.

Strangely enough, a very close friend of mine, (who I will not name because at the time, he was in a bad place), for the most part was coerced into a world he really didn't belong in. He dipped his naive toes into the disturbing world of dog fighting. This really upset me 'cos it just wasn't him: he's a nice man with a decent code of morals. But anyway, he kept on doing it, so to make him see sense I belittled him, in the hope that he would turn his back on this fackin' horrible pastime. Fackin' pastime! What a liberty it is, I reckon it's diabolical, pitting a defenceless animal against one that was seemingly ridden with rabies. I remember saying to him, 'You're a fighter, son, so why don't you get in the ring and fackin' fight? Come on ya cunt, let's see how tough you fackin' are against a snarling dog (me) off its leash!' I think it did the trick, 'cos he stepped away and has been embarrassed about it ever since. Sorry mate, but I simply needed to stress my distaste and hate for people who peddle such behaviour to the young ones out there that might be eyeing it up as a career option. It fackin' disgusts me ... and if I ever come across someone doing it (even at my age) I'll bash you up proper!

Now, here's a story for you, get on this...

Down in the deepest recesses of the prison was a right scruffy old boy, a moggy (cat). He had bad eyes: conjunctivitis

I think they call it. Well anyway, he had that, so his eyes were all sore and the lids stuck together with some sort of gunk and shit – poor bastard. He also had something wrong with his back, he walked a little strange and had to stop every few steps and have a sit down – I don't think he liked that, 'cos he wasn't that old, I think he'd just fell on hard times and ended up in the prison's sewerage system right at the base of the nick.

So, how did he get there? Well, this was a mystery to every fucker; he must've snuck in through a pipe or something; he probably got in through an open door and lost his way out, and with his eyesight so poor this was totally feasible. But who the fuck was he? Well, he was D-Cat Charlie, the prison fackin' moggy, wasn't he? Well, he was once I took him in. But, before our union he was most probably called Tiddles or something soft like that. Anyway, I adopted him, and took him away to my cell. I put cold teabags on his eyes, and it quickly cleared his eye problem up. After a while it became quite obvious that the warders weren't too keen on me keeping him, but I thought, they can go fuck themselves, 'cos this old boy needed looking after.

I learned a lot about animals from the Gypsy community; my aunt who read tea leaves being the one I took most advice from. But on this occasion, I got these little veterinary tips from some travellers who were in the nick with me. The screws also brought me a pigeon; they said a cat had had it and its back was all damaged. Anyway, these Gypsy boys told me to put him in warm water and let him swim about a bit. That way it would steadily fuse its back together. So, that's what I done … and fuck me they were bang on, 'cos the little fella started to move about like Cassius Clay (the boxer, later called Mohamed Ali): he was bobbing and weaving all over the gaff.

I kept all sorts of animals in Springhill prison. People used to fetch all the broken animals to me and I'd fix them up. Someone gave me a few greenfinches, and I made a cage for them in my woodwork class. I even had a fackin' bat ... yeah, a bat ... not a vampire one, 'cos I'd have been scared of that little fucker late at night when the lights were out. I wouldn't want that thing waking up and biting the fuck outta me Gregory (Gregory Peck – neck) nah, fuck that.

One day I managed to get on the outside of the nick, and I found an old fackin' bed. I shouted a couple of boys over and got them to help me get it back to my cell. I swapped it over with the prison issue one, and it was fantastic; it made my prison one look like something out of an old WW2 film.

It was a mental setup down there; I could basically get away with anything. I remember having this new cellmate turn up. He was okay, but he was a bit of a lunatic. He started bringing all this stuff back to our cell: compost and other garden clobber. Anyway, one day I asked him what he was going to do with it all, and he told me he was going to make a fackin' bomb. Well, as I'm sure you can imagine, I went off my fackin' nuts. 'What the fuck are you talking about you lunatic?' I asked him. 'Now you can fuck that straight off! If you think you're making bombs in my cell you've got another think coming. Now get this fackin' lot out of here, and fast!' Obviously, he did as he was told, and we moved on. Mind you, he must've been cranky or something 'cos he had already been given ten three-year sentences to run concurrently; the reason for that was I think three years was the most they could give you in a D-Cat (category) nick.

All the boys down there used to listen to Stormin' Norman, and most of the time me and my name did better work than the screws did. This one day, I was sat minding my own business on a visit with my missus at the time, Tracey, when all these fackin' Asian boys started kicking off. Eh? There were women and kids on visits in the room. So, I went fackin' nuts, and I was growling and spitting at all of them, 'Aaargh, you fackin' bunch of cunts … sit down. I've got children here … and so have these other people! You wanna play, play when you get out of prison and not in front of my children!' I was right off it, and whenever I got like that, I'd bring other people into it as well. 'You think you can outnumber the screws twenty to one? Well, ya can't outnumber me 'cos I don't give a fuck! Now, fuck you, sit the fuck down, shut up, or you'll have a hard fackin' day off me!' Immediately the whole roomful of people sat down like a classroom full of schoolchildren. Even the screws looked a little sheepish, but later thanked me for doing what they couldn't do.

But hey, they didn't have to worry, I was helping them out; I always helped them. And when the YPs were bang out of order on the landing, I'd run into the cell that they were parked up in and slap the lot of them and throw them onto the landing. And there they'd be, all embarrassed 'cos they'd had a telling-off from me. On the occasion I'm referring to, the screws fled as well. And when I'd stopped shouting at everybody, this screw came over and said, 'Bloody hell, Norman, please don't do that again, 'cos I almost pissed my fucking pants!' Anyway, I said, 'No … c'mon boss, I was just geeing them up a bit … I was just playing with them.'

But anyway, back to D-Cat Charlie for a minute...

In the end the governor of the nick got wind of our little bunk-up pussycat, and I had to hand him over to Tracey on her next visit. But honestly, I couldn't work out how they knew he was mine. So, I asked the screws and they said, 'We knew it was yours, Norm, 'cos every time we chased it, it ran under your bed.' Anyway, I handed it over to Tracey and she took it home and took care of him. Then, a little while later when I got released, he lived with us: he stayed with us for years. So, talk about the Birdman of Alcatraz. Well, for a time I was the fackin' 'Cat-man of Springhill'. Well, Cat, Bat and Bird man as well if I want to show off a bit.

In the end all of these animals in my cell started making too much noise, and some of the inmates started to complain. So, I had to hand them all over to the RSPCA. Five finches, a pigeon and a fackin' bat: it was like Whipsnade Zoo in my cell at one point ... I should've cashed in on it and charged the other inmates an entry fee to see them.

Apart from the animals and all that caper there was other stuff that went on, stuff that you never hear about in the papers or anything. I remember we had a fackin' tramp come in at Christmastime. This fella came round with the fackin' tea-trolley. Anyway, I gave him a bed for the night and asked him what was wrong, and he said it was fackin' cold outside and all he wanted was a cup of hot tea ... bless him. I told him to go down to the hut in the morning, and there he could get himself a breakfast. I told him not to go down to the dinner hut in his civvie clobber though, 'cos he'd get himself nicked. So, I dressed him up in a prison shirt and tie, and he went down and was chatting to all the cons and that and getting on with them all into the bargain.

A bit later the screws came over. They were laughing and saying, 'Ya can't do this Norm ... you'll get us lot fucking shot!' But I asked them if we could just keep hold of him for a little while longer 'cos it was fackin' freezing outside. But they said he hasn't committed a crime Norman, they said they couldn't take any old waifs and strays in, and said I'd have to tell him to leave. Anyway, I told him he could stay for a bit of dinner and tea, but he'd have to leave before lights-out. And that was that, the poor fucker had to spend the rest of the festive season outside the prison walls in the Siberian cold. Mind you he had managed to blag it, he'd had a good old nosh-up, all dressed up in his HMP clobber, and enjoyed the warmth indoors for a day or two. He was a lovely geezer, and it made me happy thinking that he'd had a nice time with me over the Christmas period.

11

THE GUV'NOR'S PORRIDGE

Writers' Note
*While wading through a light portion of porridge, our man Stormin'
Norman lapped up a sense of responsibility, as he guided many a failing
young offender to a more righteous and honourable path.*

There were some right faces in the nick. I remember a man I
have a lot of time for, John, John Stanley; strangely enough I
went to his Aunty Renie's funeral recently and he spotted me
straight away and came over and thanked me for attending,
and we had a nice little chat about the old days. The Old Bill
were there as well, they didn't make a fuss though, I don't
think they had the fackin' nerve to. But they stayed close by
and watched on from behind a wall. I remember someone
saying, 'I wonder if one of those soppy cunts will give me a
lift home.'

Another proper hard nut with a big reputation who was
in Springhill was Dan Rooney, the Gypsy fighter. Now, he
was a big geezer, and a tough, tough man too. Sometime in
the early 1990s a bare-knuckle fight was secretly filmed over
in a little village called Crossmaglen in Northern Ireland.
Rooney's opponent was another traveller known as Aney

McGinley. Apparently, the two families had had a dispute and Dan wanted to settle their disagreement over a 'fair-go' as they call it. (A fair-go is a toe-to-toe fight using fists and no villainy.)

If I remember right, Lenny McLean did the voice-over on the video. I've never seen it, but the boys tell me it was a good old traditional Gypsy scrap. However, due to Rooney making the other geezer wait for him to turn up, it kicked off with the supporters and the Old Bill tried to put a stop to it – according to McLean the authorities were politely told to get on their fackin' bikes.

As I said in the last chapter, when I was in prison, I basically ran the place; everyone respected me and everyone left me alone. I'd have my laundry done for me, all folded up nice, and they would even throw in a few new tracksuits for me when they brought my clobber back to my cell. For me, it was like a fackin' hotel. But I always had great respect for everyone, and, just as in my normal life, I never took liberties.

Before I got locked up, me and the missus pulled up at the side of Stevan one day in the car, and he said, while laughing his head off, 'Fucking hell Norm ... I thought you was Starsky and Hutch just then!' (This was a popular cops and robbers TV programme at the time.) Mind you I wasn't always the loveable lunatic, and one day while in prison I ended up banging out one of the screws. 'Ere listen...

Another thing I remember happening inside. Every day all through the day the youngsters would make me cups of tea and I used to love it, it made me feel well respected. Then one day I went to make a cuppa for one of the youngsters and when I opened my box of teabags, there was only about six left: the little bastards had got a razor blade and cut a hole out the back of my tea box! I could see the fuckers laughing, at which point I realised they had been making the tea for me with my own fackin' bags, and there was me thinking they were being generous ... cheeky little fuckers! But hey, it was all for laughs, and I still loved them all to pieces.

Like in most prisons, not many of the inmates get on very well with the staff, but me I was different, I didn't mind 'em. Look, the way I see it is the screws are just doing their jobs, much the same as me when I was doing my job working the doors. You know how it is, not many people like bouncers either, 'cos we're keeping the unruly fuckers in line, and they don't fackin' like it. And like I say, I was different: I took them as I found them. Yeah, some of them can be corrupt cunts who are out for themselves, but you just play those ones for what you can get out of them as well. But aside from that, you keep ya' distance from them and watch from the sidelines, 'cos they always manage to fuck it up for themselves in the end, and then you can laugh at them for taking liberties.

As I say these geezers have a job to do, and when they used to ship one lot of YPs out, they'd then have to ship a new lot in, and immediately, the new lot would play up. There would be bullies among them, and the obvious troublemakers, and these fuckers would give the other YPs a bit of a hard time. Then, the screws would come to me and ask me to have a word with them ... ya know ... calm the fuckers down and bring a bit of peace to the place. You see, it's not a very nice environment for some of 'em, and they have a hard time getting used to it and settling in. And, whenever there was a turnaround of YPs, the suicides and attempted suicides would rocket, and, in turn, this would give the prison and the governor a bad name. So, being the nice geezer I am, I would help them out a bit; I'd step in and growl a bit.

When I was on B Wing, I got it all down to a tee. I knew how to use my voice with the screams and the growling, and, like I said, at times even some of the screws would shit themselves. One day I went in and I started screaming to about eight youngsters who were lined up – I gave them a right fackin' telling off, I started shouting, 'Right, this is my manor now … this is my wing, these are my fackin' rules and there will be no more bullying! This is my set of rules and if you don't like it, you can all fuck off!' To be honest, I don't know where they were going to fuck off to, but I had hijacked the wing and before I knew it, I was having my clothes washed and ironed and was well looked after. And because I kept the place under control, even the screws left me alone. 'Cos let's face it, I was basically doing something they couldn't. Mind you, I was always polite to the screws, and they liked me because of my old-fashioned approach.

At the end of the day, I love everyone, and I will help them if they need me. I like to teach the young people the ways of the world, 'cos when I was growing up I was very naive, and I had to learn things the hard way. I had an extremely cruel and hard life and never liked some of the things I had to do. So, with the wisdom I had gained through the years, I'd put it across to the youngsters to get their heads down – do their time – and have respect for the screws, even if they didn't like some of them. I'd also tell them to toe the line, 'cos there was no way on this earth that they could ever beat the system. Like I said, I always respected the officials and I got on great with them.

At one point during my porridge, I was going through bad times as my wife had said she wanted to divorce me. Anyway, late one night, one of the screws came into my cell, sat on the end of the bed, and asked if I was alright. He was really concerned for me, and it meant a lot having someone on the other side of the fence that I could talk to.

There was also a female screw, she was quite a bit older than me, so I used to call her Mum. She was a lovely woman. I remember one time, the screws came in to search my cell and she went absolutely ballistic at them; she went fackin' crazy, screaming at them, and ordering them out of my cell. She was curious, asking how they dared do such a thing to me! I couldn't believe it, a female screw sticking up for yours-truly. She was lovely and wouldn't have a bad word said against me.

Sometimes in prison, and probably due to my depression that came and went, the other side of my personality would come out. And out of nowhere that beast inside that showed no mercy would appear. By this time in my life, I knew how to keep the beast on a leash, because if I didn't it could get right out of hand, which was part of the reason I was in the prison in the first fackin' place. Sometimes, I would blame the steroids for the beast and its rage and anger, and when I look back, I wish I had never taken the fackin' things, and let's face it, they probably made my depression worse. But as I keep saying, at that time of life I just didn't give a fuck. Fortunately, my stay in prison did me the world of good. It helped make me see the light and taught me how my actions on the outside would often have serious and damning consequences.

It was Christmas Day 1994 in Woodhill, and all the boys were downhearted, ya know, struggling with the thought of not being able to spend time with their families and loved ones and stuff. Anyway, I was sat in my cell thinking how to cheer them all up, when, bang, it came to me, and I thought, eh, there's one geezer I can bring into the nick who is everybody's favourite uncle … yeah, you got it: Santa. And the fantastic thing was, it was easy to arrange.

So, I took a bed sheet and made it into a sack, then I used a pillowcase to wear as a big white beard. I filled the sack up with pillows and anything I could lay my hands on, then I walked out onto the landing shouting (in my best Santa voice … but just a bit more growly) Oh – Oh – Fackin' – Oh! But that wasn't enough for The Guv'nor, I couldn't leave it there. So, I stormed down the stairs hitting all the inmates with my big, massive makeshift Santa sack. Well, it definitely did the trick, 'cos Matt Legg and all the boys (who earlier were a bit downhearted) were laughing at the top of their fackin' voices; even the warders were joining in. Mind you, on another occasion I did wrap a sheet around my head like a turban and came out from my cell with a big fackin' ghetto-blaster on my shoulder, banging out Bhangra style records while doing an impression of that Bin Laden nutter. I don't think they'd take too kindly to that these days though, do you? It wasn't altogether very PC, now was it?

One of the screws, called Tommo, was one of the good ones. He was the screw who every jail should employ. He was straight with you and fair and was a bit of a handful himself. I know this because years after he came to work with me over in Wolverton.

Tommo was certainly no slouch, he'd looked after all the big names in the criminal underworld. One name that echoed through any prison like a bad smell back in those days was the infamous Charlie Bronson, or the artist reborn, Charlie Salvador, as he is now known. Coincidentally, Lee Wuff-Wuff (I always call him that, basically because I don't know how to pronounce Wortley) has just released a book called *Bronson and Me*, that he wrote about Charlie with Charlie's late wife

Paula Williamson. The book can be purchased from all good bookstores. Right, there's a good plug for your book, mate, now can we get back to the story...

Oh, fackin' hell, what was I rabbiting on about? Oh yeah, that's right, my good pal Tommo.

Right, so Tommo looked after Charlie over in Woodhill. Anyway, Charlie had lost his cool one day and ordered to see the governor. But because he'd issued a few threats they sent Tommo along for back-up. I remember Tommo saying that when they entered the cell, Charlie was stood side-on to Tommo; Tommo's arse was twitching but he had to keep his cool and make sure Charlie didn't twig; Charlie had his head down and this made Tommo a bit twitchy with the thought of Charlie suddenly exploding and bashing him up. Fortunately, that wasn't to be, 'cos Charlie said his piece, got a bit of a result, and calmed right down. You see the way I see it, this was all down to my pal Tommo and the way he treats inmates: he's honest, fair and straight, and he also says it how it is. And in prison that goes a long way. Tommo would always get good results. He's a good man is Tommo.

I remember one day I was feeling a bit aggie (full of aggression due to my dyslexia), and as I walked into the library I picked up a table and threw it across the room. Tommo ran over and asked what was wrong and I told him I get a bit upset sometimes 'cos I can't read as quickly and easily as your average Joe. Fortunately, I was sent to see the prison's optician; he prescribed me some blue-lensed glasses, and two days later I walked back into that library, and my reading inadequacy wasn't as severe. I couldn't read perfectly, but the words made a lot more sense than they had ever done before. Tommo was happy for me, as he knew my dyslexia had been getting me down.

12

MINDING MR BIG

Writers' Note

In the late1980s, late-night parties in secret locations for ravers went from strength to strength. This was the summer of 1989, when acid house parties were quickly rebranded as rave parties, and publicly schooled entrepreneurs were extremely eager to cash in on this revolutionary and lucrative new scene. The partygoers with their whistles and dummies were there waiting in the wings, and the acid dealers were just as eager to relieve them of their hard-earned wonga. And it was here where, for the promise of a few hours of escapism, this amalgamation was born. And a disused and retired old aircraft hangar, filled with the sound of a souped-up 909 bass drum, while a Kory M1 piano, hammer-riffed graciously over the top, was ample allure with which to beckon the cocked-and-ready revellers.

'Aciiiiiid! Fackin' hell, if I wasn't sick of hearing that down me' ear'oles all the time!'

It was at around this time that acid house's 'Mr Big', Tony Colston-Hayter, and his sidekick Paul Staines, the publicist and self-proclaimed Malcolm McLaren to the rave scene, had a company shake up, and renamed their illegitimate underground company as Sunrise. Then, soon afterwards, they asked my brother Alfie if our little firm of muscle would take care of their gates and all its tripping for their underground parties that went on until the wee small hours. But fuck me, the stuff we were doing was small fry compared to the shit that this conning little fucker was up to behind the scenes. Apparently, through the years, Tony and his associate cheated people out of over a million quid, but until it was splashed all over the national papers, I didn't have a fackin' clue about it.

I heard years later that this Staines geezer had invented some machine that looked like something out of the film *Back to the Future*, which helped him and Tony fool people by making them think that they were the customers' bank provider. Apparently, they used this device to get access to over a million quid from people's personal accounts, which had a knock-on effect for hundreds of people across the UK. Fackin' hell, I thought they were just a pair of Hooray Henries with cash on tap from Mummy and Daddy. How fackin' wrong could I have been? Anyway, a while before all this caper, when Tony was just a slip of a lad, I started working for him doing all-sorts. But I'll have to go back a little bit further for that, so...

In the early 1980s Tony was little more than a fackin' boy; a boy, I might add, who had his fingers and thumbs in everything that might one day bring him in a king's ransom. He was just that kind of fella: anything he could find an angle to earn a pound note in, he'd have a slice of it. And back then it was fruit machines, or slot machines as they're known around the country. Well, he had them, and he'd stick them in any place that had plenty of human traffic in and out of its doors day and night: laundrettes, cab offices, cafés, you name it, he had a fruit machine lodging in his motor, that was parked up nearby. Anyway, Tony employed me to go around these places with him watching his back as he emptied the machines and divvied out a percentage to the owner; pocketing the majority of the dough into his own bin (pocket). This was a right productive little game, and he earned a packet from it – enough dough for him to move up the ranks as fast as his dirty cash could take him.

Prior to this though, I minded him at the casinos, where this sharp little fucker used to fleece the money moguls who ran these places using their already laundered ill-gotten gains. I think he thought he was helping them out; I think he believed he was playing his part in laundering it for them, yet all the time pocketing some of it himself as he played blackjack while 'counting cards' with dazzle-eyed acumen right under their fackin' noses. This geeky bohemian was as brazen as a hooker down Gropecunt Lane. I mean, you never get away with it forever, and sometimes it would get a bit heavy, so that's why he had muggins here taking care of him in case it ever got a bit naughty. I mean, I didn't always agree with him, but he treated me well, and upped the digits on me bank balance a fair bit.

This one night, we were down the casino. Obviously, Tony's there doing what he does best, but this other fella – a minder – is non-stop whispering in his governor's ear; he obviously knows what Tony's doing and is trying to put a fackin' block on him. Anyway, I've clocked this nosey fucker, and I've given him a look that said, I've got your number, you cunt! But he took no pissing notice and kept on with the whispering; whatever he was whispering to his governor was obviously getting his boss rattled, 'cos he's got his eyes fixed firmly on Tony, all menacing. But I'm guessing it's attracting a bit of attention from the owners and I'm thinking, this cunt needs pulling.

By this point I'd seen enough, this geezer was about to get us pinched, and the owner's going to ask Tony to leave, and because of this silly cunt I'm about to lose me fackin' bonus. 'Fuck that,' I thought, 'this cunt needs a telling off.' So I've nodded over to him (all smiles and smokescreens) to meet me outside the club. Anyway, I wasn't in the mood for chatting, so, as soon as we stepped outside, I've hit him ... *crack* ... right in the fackin' eye, and my signature ring, the big leery one you've probably seen in photos, has split his eye wide open and the cunt's shouting and yelling like I've fackin' shot him or something. With that I've strutted back into the main room and quietly whispered to his governor, ''Ere mate, your pal's on the deck outside. I think he's been mugged by a couple of scallies.' With that the governor's shot up, asked the croupier, or whatever ya call him, to take care of his chips, and he's had it away on his toes as well.

Tony was into the gaff for about 30k (£30,000) at this point, so, knowing my wedge would be a hefty bag-and-a-half (bag of sand – grand, meaning £1500), I've whispered to him and given him the full SP (the entire background story), and told him to cash up a bit lively 'cos we needed to get out of the place. Strangely enough, I never saw that geezer there again, the minder I mean, his governor was always there, sat in the same fackin' seat, only now he had a new minder in tow with a little less fackin' attitude. To this day I don't know what his problem was, I thought people like us were supposed to look after each other, weren't we? He must've been jealous of Tony or something and looking back I wouldn't have blamed him – 'cos Tony was a proper clever, leery bastard.

So anyway, our little firm started working for Mr Big in the late 1980s; it was 1989, I think. At the time, Tony was big news, he was on the news a lot and they were saying he was some big entrepreneur. He was also on TV programmes presented by Jonathan Ross and his brother Paul. He was on a show called *One Hour* one night, and he got up and handcuffed himself to Jonathan. Jonathan took it in good humour, although to be honest, I don't think that little stunt did him, Tony, any favours.

A couple of days later, I was out with my old pal Henry Simpson. ('Ere, don't you go telling him I called him old, 'cos he'll be after me!) Anyway, I was just in the middle of telling him about the casino fiasco when he asked if I knew a particular geezer whom I won't name. Well, for obvious reasons I ain't gonna float the geezer's name about, am I, 'cos his family are still active. So, for the purposes of this next bit, let's just say his name was Barry M. Look, it's as easy as eggs: I don't want to have to come out of retirement on account of some rabbiting I've done that has raked up a load of shit for the geezers involved.

Anyway, I'd only just finished my stretch at Woodhill, so I was feeling a bit mellow, well, not exactly mellow, but let's just say I was being a bit careful. Listen, I'd only just returned home to my family, and the last thing I needed was to get myself another long holiday in the clink. Anyway, Henry explained to me that he had been challenged with some little problem and was hoping I wanted to help him solve it. Henry knew I would be treading a bit careful, but he also knew that I needed to feed my family. And anyway, as I've mentioned many times in past chapters, Henry is a very clever fella, and it was obvious to me that if he was involved, I'd be on to a winner; this man was nothing if he wasn't meticulous.

Here's the briefing…

Some geezers had threatened a very dear friend of Henry's. This little firm had said that the geezer's family would be bang in trouble if Mr M didn't cough up 100 big ones (£100,000). This was just a straightforward ransom gig, ya know, you line our pockets with a bag of folding, and we won't torture your fackin' family and whatever else. It was a right naughty little racket, and back in the 1980s every fucker was at it. If you think about it, it's a no-brainer; it's the easiest and quickest way to grab a nice bit of dough without having to pull up any trees. It was almost a guarantee, 'cos the victim (in this case Mr M) was loaded, and due to the fact that he liked to have his greedy little digits in everything that promised a few quid (including naughty little moody ventures on the other side of the fence) he was fair game. And the last thing he wanted was the Flying Squad sniffing around his business premises and properties, and fuck me, did this geezer have some bricks and mortar in his portfolio. However, Henry had an ace up his sleeve, because his contact, Mr M, had handed him some paperwork that would land this firm's boss in a whole host of trouble. (Think Cynthia Payne and her naughty little house of pleasure, and you won't be far off the mark.)

Right, so this was 'The Professor's' (Henry's) plan…

Henry would set up a meet with the boss of this little firm. He'd show him a copy of the detrimental evidence and get him to call the dogs off of his pal. In turn, Mr M would be off the leash, and Henry and my good self would be into him for a tidy few quid; not to mention a bit of a pension as security for making sure no one else tries coming-it with a similar move. (Pension: concurrent reparations for services rendered.)

And it's on…

Henry rolls up at our designated meeting place, beeps his horn, and I jump in the passenger seat. But Henry ain't his usual happy-go-lucky self. ''Ello mate ... what's wrong?' I enquire immediately. 'Poxy, bloody Crown Green Bowling ... that's what's up, Norm.' He replied, sounding as if he had the hump. 'Crown Green fackin' Bowling?' I yelled. 'What the hell is that all about?' 'Yes Norm,' Henry went on. 'This chap (the big boss) rang me earlier and said, "Oh sorry, I forgot: I'm practising today, bowling! I have a cup game on Sunday, and today is the only free day I have for the next few weeks. You did say you needed to see me urgently, so, could we meet there? Oh, and don't worry, it'll be just me and my driver down there."'

'Well, that's okay isn't it, Henry?' I said. 'I wouldn't mind having a play with some of those wooden ball things.' And Henry replied, 'Well yes, but you interrupted me, and I didn't get a chance to finish. Yes, the bowling isn't the problem ... I just didn't plan on driving all the way down to Brighton for the bloody day, did you?!' 'Oh, fackin' hell, Brighton,' I said, 'that's about five fackin' hours away, isn't it?' 'Well not quite that far, Norm ... but we'd better get our clog (shoe) down ... I've got another meet at three.' And off we went.

We arrived in Brighton in good time. Henry had a lovely motor back then – dead cosy. Anyway, I was just dozing off when the anchors went on, and Henry hollered, 'Right son, wake up ... we're here.'

Fackin' hell, that startled me a bit – and I was thinking to myself, I'd better liven myself up, we've got work to do, as I eased myself out of the lovely warm seat. I'm sure Henry warms those seats up on purpose; I think he does it to piss me off when he knows I'm all comfy, knowing I'll have to leap out into the cold at a moment's notice. He's a clever git is our

'Enry. Anyway, I could see we were only seconds away from the meet, 'cos I spotted the bowls place just a few hundred feet away. And we're walking...

Henry walks straight over to the boss man, while I introduce myself to his driver, quickly realising that this was no driver; this geezer was muscle. More to the point, I already knew him: I sparred with him years ago, and we became good pals. So, I said to him, "Ere Tel, (Terry was his name) these cunts who work for your guvnor are bang out of order ... strongin' it with my guvnor's boss: threatening his family and that is a fackin' death wish ... Are they the full ticket or what?' And Tel said, 'Between you and me, Norm, it's his son: he's a fucking wrong-un! He's tried the same with a few firms. But listen, my guvnor is ready to offload him. So as long as your guvnor and mine hit it off, everything will be sweet.' And just as Tel had finished speaking, I looked up, caught Henry's eye and he winked, giving me the nod to say it was boxed-off. Then I nodded back, pointed at Tel, and gave him the thumbs up. Sorted! Tel and I had a quick chat, swapped numbers, and arranged to meet up at a boxing do in a few weeks' time ... and that was that, we left the place. Mind you, I was a bit cheesed-off that I never even got the chance to do a bit of bowling, I reckon I'd have been good at it. Having said that, I'd forgotten my cue anyway!

So, the job was done, the dogs had been well and truly called off. Henry said it was like selling oil to Arabs; he said Tel's boss was going to drop Henry's guvnor the word, and also say that Henry should be well looked after for his intervention. (I never saw Henry invent fuck-all, as it goes!) We had a stroll down the promenade, I ate my body weight in cockles and mussels, and it was alive-alive-oh, and we were on our way 'ome.

Joking apart, Henry bunged me a nice wedge (undisclosed, you nosey fuckers ... you might work for the Inland fackin' Revenue) and we shot off home. Oh, and we got there two hours earlier than anticipated, which meant our 'Enry was his usual happy-go-lucky self again.

13

DOWN THE BARN: TEAR-UPS AND
FLARE-UPS

Writers' Note

If you think you've got what it takes, get down the barn! If you think that boxing in a ring is soppy, safe and easy, get down the barn. However, if you want to turn your life on a sixpence; if you're willing to let a once off-the-rails British Bulldog school you in the art of morality, while gifting you a Guv'nor-sized serving of self-belief, get down the barn.

'Tear-ups and Flare-ups...'

Sounds like something from one of them Guy Ritchie Brit flicks, doesn't it? Hey, but listen, that was how it was down the barn: this place was no fackin' film set, it was blood, sweat and fear for whoever ventured in there. This place at the back of my garden was where it all happened. To be honest though, it did look like some set of a film, with an old caravan with half its door missing, and an old boxing ring fit for a good old row parked up in the middle. Not to mention the handful of boxing bags that were dangling on chains from the rusty fackin' rafters. Where, in and amongst all the normal ones, lurked a rogue bag that was full to the brim with bits of concrete and masonry. And when some young likely lad full of piss, wind and attitude walked in, I would listen carefully as he ambled his way over to the bag of bricks and smash it with his hardest hook, and I'd be stood there pissing myself, laughing at his screams for his mummy. What? I ain't wicked … I just don't like cocky little cunts whose confidence has a louder voice than his ability! Mind you, don't tell them, but I even laughed at some of my good pals when they got turned over by that great rock-filled swindler.

Joking apart, I had loads of little battles in that place: Gypsies would bring their top men down to see if they had the stuff to go at it with me. But every time they stepped between the ropes I'd give them a quick sharp-shock lesson in how not to challenge The Guv'nor in his own backyard. Still, they never learned, and they'd be back a few days later with another wannabe lunatic who needed a schooling in the art of pugilistic ruling. Mind you, it wasn't all about showing the local hard men who was boss; I did a lot of good in there, too.

You see sometimes, some local boy who was getting bullied, or some little ruffian who thought he liked the idea of straying from the path of righteousness, would be marched down by his father to see me, and his father would plead with me to put his son to work in the barn, praying to the gods that I could sift out the badness from within him – and it worked – almost every time. On many occasions I turned a bitter and bad apple into a rosy red tasty one, and I fackin' revelled in it; I saw it as a great achievement. It mustered up a sense of inner pride. Not to mention the fact that I felt I was giving a little back to the community.

Talking about making people feel good about themselves…

One day in the Agora, I spotted this young boy all on his lonesome sat in the café. He looked like he never had a pot to piss in as he gazed across at the food and cakes on the other customers' plates. He looked proper down on his luck and to be honest, he reminded me of myself when I was a young boy. Anyway, I pulled a tenner out of my wallet and slipped it in my pocket, then I got myself a cuppa tea then slowly walked past where he was sat. Then, without him noticing, I dropped the tenner on the deck near his feet. 'Ere son,' I told him, 'I'd watch yourself, you've just dropped a tenner on the floor … I'd pick it up a bit lively before someone has it away.' He looked at me all puzzled. 'There, look!' I said, nodding to his feet, 'it's right near your foot … you don't wanna lose that … 'cos I bet your mum will go off her nut!' He looked around a bit, then bent down, picked it up, and said, 'Thank you … it's my dinner money for the week … Mum will kill me if I lose it, it's the last of her wages!' Poor little sod, I thought to myself. I bet he ain't had a nice bit of grub in ages. With that, I went to the counter, got him a cream bun and big strawberry milkshake, and said, ''Ere son, I won't tell your mum you took something off a stranger if you don't.' He nodded his head vigorously in agreement. 'You're not a stranger. You're Norman the bouncer, you look after people.'

That made me feel great, it's nice to know that the young ones trust me, especially in this day and age. Anyway, I asked him what he was doing on his own and, ever so reluctantly, he told me that some boys were after him and that the café was the only place where he knew he'd be safe. Fackin' bullying bastards, now he really does remind me of a young me. So anyway, I sat in the seat opposite and we started chatting. I asked him if he liked boxing and immediately, he came right out of his shell talking about Mike Tyson, Frank Bruno, Lennox Lewis, all the heavyweights. This young boy knew 'em all; he even knew all the fights they'd had, and which ones they had won and lost. Fuck me, he even taught me a thing or two about who's who in the game.

So, I asked him if the boys always picked on him and told him that I used to get picked on as well. He couldn't believe his ears, and said I was too big for anybody to hit. But I told him, yes, I am now, son, but when I was a young boy, I was just like him, and everyone had a go at me. I told him that I got bullied right up until I learned how to box, and that if he squared it up with his mum and dad, I would train him to box just like me. Well, his little face lit up. And with that, he thanked me for the bun, and said he was off home to ask his mum if she would fetch him down the barn. And the very next day they turned up at my barn and I taught him how to look after himself. As luck would have it, he turned out to be a natural, but he was just too frightened to have a go back. He said that he'd never even thrown a punch till he came to the barn, and that he didn't even know if he could. Well, that myth was soon history, 'cos he had a fantastic right-hook on him. And eventually the boy done good, when he went on to fight in some local schoolboy competitions, and believe it or not, he was never bullied again.

I used to love training the young ones down the barn. I'd get 'em gloved up and in the ring with me and they'd bash the hell out of my belly. They'd smash their best shots at me and would love it if they thought I was hurting. Siobhan, my daughter, used to watch, and she'd laugh and shout, 'Watch out, Dad ... he's after you!' The young boys loved it and would get all hyper at the thought of beating me. For me this was really what the barn was all about; it was a place to realise your worth; a place to make you feel good, make you feel alive and powerful like nothing in life could hurt you.

Well, that's how I saw it, and I hope the young people who attended felt that way too.

We used to get all sorts of people down the barn. You'd get Gypsy boys with their hangers-on who fancied trying their luck, and wannabe gangsters who wanted a bit of a ruck. And because it looked so rough and ready, you would get film producers down there hoping to use it for scenes in their films. But most times we would just get simple everyday folk who just wanted to tell their pals they had spent a bit of time with yours-truly. That's not me being a bighead, it was just common knowledge. Because these geezers would have their picture taken with me, and then post it all over the Internet, with the tag: 'I met The Guv'nor ... Stormin' Norman'. Listen, there are more photos out there of geezers I've never met until the day the photo was taken doing a fist bump with me than you could ever imagine. I bet every man and his fackin' dog has a picture of my big ugly growling mug hung discreetly on a wall someplace in their home where their missus won't give them too much earache. My missus wouldn't have it! Some big fucker with a face like a bulldog splashed all over her palace walls? You gotta be joking! Not on your fackin' nelly! Anyway, back to the barnies down the barn...

I remember one Sunday afternoon quite vividly when a bunch of likely lads turned up full of coke and booze. These fuckers wanted a row, and I was right in the mood to accommodate 'em. There they were taking the piss out of a few of the youngsters on the bags, so I said to one of the young boys, "'Ere son, get yourself over on the bag o' death. 'Ere, watch how you hit it though, remember it's rock fackin' solid! Listen, just shadow box it but make out you're putting a bit of a shift in. Ya know, make it look like you're hitting it hard. Then sit back and watch the show.'

So, he does as I said, and he's on it. He's doing a good job as well, making all the usual boxer noises, huffing, puffing and spitting through his nose like a pro. Suddenly, these three idiots are distracted by him and are looking over at him while taking the piss, as they're shadow boxing each other where they were stood. Then, one of them, a big mouthy Yorkshire sounding cunt shouted, 'Well go on lad, don't tickle the 'fing … Fucking hit it!' And I shouted back in reply on the boy's behalf: 'He's only a boy … get yourself over there and show him how it's done. 'Ere, a big lump like you will bust it wide open, don't you reckon?' And with that, the soppy fucker took the bait…

Anyway, he waltzed over like he was cock of the walk. He took his coat off and slung it on the deck. Then, he got himself in a two-bit boxer's stance, and unloaded a massive combo of shots into it. And after the slightest of pauses he screamed at the top of his lungs, just like a dog being doctored without anaesthetic! This fucker was in agony: his knuckles were bust up to fuck and he was screaming and bawling all the way out of my barn. His pal opened the passenger side door of his car, they got in, and sped off down the road with his pal driving. Broken, deflated and embarrassed, and with two broken bones for his trouble. That'll teach you to come down my barn all boozed-up and leery I thought as I stood there laughing, thinking, well, those clowns won't be back in a fackin' hurry.

14

WATCH MY BACK, GUV

Writers' Note

When you're a minder, it's all about reputation, and losing some row with another firm's henchman will very quickly see you demoted to the bodyguards' graveyard. This was never on the cards for Norman, he stood firm and took on all-comers. His MO (Modus Operandi – the way he works) always being: 'Not a soul around, can ever take my crown.'

It isn't easy being a tough guy. There's always a geezer out there who wants you to do his dirty work for a swift fackin' handshake and a pocketful of promises! You see, half of them don't wanna pay a proper bit of dough for your services. Look, most of these faceless, feckless office-boys want you to go in, all guns blazing, pull a massive amount of scratch in for them and bung you what they consider to be a drink, to which I'd say: 'Listen 'ere son, my kitchen sink (drink) must be a lot bigger than your one, 'cos by the look of the lack of folding you're holding, I'm getting the stark impression you only want to give me enough dough to fill up my petrol tank and have it away in ya' slinky Louis Vuitton Manhattans. Well, not on your fackin' nelly sunshine. 'Cos for the kind of dangerous places you want me lurking about in, it's gonna cost ya …

and I mean fackin' COST YOU! Now, get ya' hands deep down in ya' skyrockets (pockets) and pay me what I'm due! Otherwise, it's you I'm gonna be falling out with!'

These fuckers always try to beeswax (tax) my hard-earned bit o' scratch. Fackin' greedy bastards these businessmen: it's always something' for nuffin with 'em! As long as they've got a bit o' poppy (money) left over to buy their bit on the side a nice bit of Tom they're happy! Well, I ain't happy, so I'd say, now grease my palm with a nice hefty bit of dough. And once you show them who's boss, they quickly come round to your way of thinking.

So-and-so's minding such-and-such, this fella looks after this other geezer, this fella's under this other fella's wing, and who am I looking after? No cunt; well, that's given me the needle straight away. Right, do your homework Norm, have a word in the right ear: pull the right chain and your minding days to the stars will soon be underway.

But was it that easy? Was it bollocks!

I was working up in Birmingham for a man called Vic Bellamy. He's a promoter and businessman, not to mention being a big fucker himself...

Anyway, Vic had got himself into a bit of bother with a well-known Scottish gangland enforcer called Billy McPhee; the word on the street was that he'd been sent down to put it on my guv'nor, Vic. This McPhee fella was himself a total lunatic, and according to 'the chaps' he was known to be one of the hardest men in Scotland: an unbeaten force on the street. In addition to that, it was also said that he had killed at least eight people in gangland hits, and apparently he had been shot in the face as a result of one of these hits a short time before our meet.

From what I remember, McPhee came down from Scotland to where I was minding a door. There was some sort of business deal going on, and McPhee wasn't happy, which fuelled him to offer out all the doormen for a tear-up. However, due to McPhee's fearsome reputation, the other men shied away from the challenge, and the only one to accept was me.

Anyway, he came at me like a lunatic, so I smashed him with a three or four punch combination, and, although he was dazed and a little confused, the man just stood there looking at me and said in his broad Scottish brogue that would have made The Hulk squirm, 'Oh, so yous a fackin' boxer is ye?' At this point it was obvious to me that this was going to be a bit of a hefty tear-up. And it was.

As we fought, toe-to-toe, this McPhee geezer kept growling like a rabid dog; it was fackin' nasty, eyes were gouged, bollocks got bitten, this tear-up went on and on. Eventually I started to swing the crazy fucker around by his hair, and seconds later I'd managed to dislocate his neck, and that was the end of that! I'd finally seen-off one of Scotland's finest henchmen; but suddenly, out of the blue he walked over to me and tried shaking my hand. I thought, are you fucking joking? I don't trust this fucker! So, I stuck the nut into him for good measure. He looked at me in disbelief; I suppose he thought he'd met his raving-lunatic match.

I heard later that this McPhee bloke actually said it was the first time he'd ever been beaten in a fight. Mind you, this madman was destined for a life of pain, 'cos a few years later a hit was ordered and sent out to some extra naughty lunatic in the east end of Scotland, and, as he stood at the bar in a family-packed Brewers Fayre on a relaxing Sunday afternoon, he was set upon, beaten-up, and stabbed-up some twenty-seven times in a frenzied killing. Apparently, McPhee had wounds all over his body, from his head to his ankles – even his meat and two fuckin' veg were sliced up.

The merchandise wars, as they call them, weren't any easier, 'cos this little battle brought trouble from all the major cities in the UK...

You see, everybody paid for their bit of merchandise to take centre stage at a certain event venue, and whoever threw the most pound notes in the event organiser's bin, got the best pitch and promotion. Anyway, that's where people like me get hired in: we were simply hired muscle to keep things sweet, and if someone didn't play ball, we'd have to get hands-on heavy with them.

It could be a right ball-ache at times 'cos everyone had their own little firm of minders, and these boys were coming down tooled up (with weapons) to put the squeeze on any other firms, just like we were paid to do. I remember one night a big blue tranny (Ford Transit) van-load of these heavies turned up, but before they had a chance to leave their seats, get out of the van and get busy, I went loopy, like a raving lunatic, smashing at their windows and hollering at them to dare to get out and see what happened to them. Fortunately for me, they didn't have enough arsehole between them and so swiftly did a U-turn. Which was fackin' fortunate really, 'cos I was strongin' it a bit! I mean who the fuck did I think I was, pissing Hercules or something?

Which reminds me, one day 'Our 'Enry' gave me a call-up...

No, calm down, it's not the one you're thinking of, the legendary boxer Henry Cooper, but he's every bit as much of a winner in my eyes. He's every bit the same steadfast geezer built from the great British stock of pre-war Britain. But no, I'm talking about my pal ... or who I think of as my second dad, Henry Simpson, or 'The Professor' as he is more reverently known.

'Morning my good man,' he said. 'I have a little job for you … it's a nice little earner, and a nice little jaunt up the coast.'

Well, it sounded like a nice day out, so I jumped at it. 'Right, where you taking me, and what's the bit of work, Dad?' I asked, hoping for an easy day with big pay. But no, it's never that easy, cool ya' boots Norm, I thought, you know only too well that when you expect champagne, life has a tendency to give you rancid, sour grapes. But fuck it, I needed a few quid, and like our trip up to Brighton, everything The Professor is wrapped around always has a good bit of dough on offer. So I'm off, down the Agora for a quick bacon roll and a measure of the job and its itinerary. Apparently, he's phoned McLean but he's busy, so I'm second best and ready for a bit of a wind-up.

'So … Lenny on his way down is he 'Enry?' I asked as I ordered my stuff from the waitress at the counter while giving her a bit of Guv'nor charm. 'Enry looked at me all puzzled, turning his head to look around like a paranoid barn owl. 'Lenny?' Henry enquired. 'Why who said anything about Lenny, Norman?' 'Well not you, Dad,' I told him, 'but I heard on the grapevine that McLean's turned you down and I'm coming off the subs bench to take his place. Or have I got that wrong?' With that, 'Enry twigged the wind-up and chased me round the café like a boy about to be caned by the headmaster. 'Sorry Dad,' I explained, 'I just wanted to see if I could liven you up a bit, 'cos usually, it's the other way round.'

Anyway, we had a bit of a laugh and a joke, and then 'Enry filled me in on what the score was. He proceeded to tell me that he wanted the two of us on this little number, but Lenny was at a big meet at Heathrow Airport, so he's got another geezer meeting us at the other end who will fill in for Lenny's absence.

Right, so the job was down the coast in Clacton – kiss-me-quick hats and hotdogs – that'll do me. Apparently, some ex-prize-fighter (no names) took the money on the door at a Scottish gangster's boxing event and had it away on his toes with the night's takings; not to mention nicking the raffle money that was for some local charity. Fortunately, though, the dough wasn't for some poor fucker on their last-legs, 'cos fuck me, that would've been a death warrant. Apparently, this mobster up the cold-end (Scotland) wasn't at all happy and wanted the boxer, and (or) the dough, brought to him, for, well, let's just say retribution, the poor fucker! So, it's a good few bob, and a free pass to Glasgow's night life for me and our 'Enry, if, or should I say *when*, we get a result. I'm in and we're off.

During our journey up the coast, I asked 'Enry who this prize-fighting geezer was, and what he has to offer. 'Enry quickly informed me that the geezer, who was now in his late forties, was still a tasty geezer but was way past his best. He then said that, for added security, he's worded his pal up in Clacton to park up outside the place we're heading to, just in case it got a bit lively. Because like 'Enry said, this fella might have a few hangers-on, and our man is coming-it like he's the Great Gatsby and serving up the cash to them. And for that matter, these fellas might not like the idea of the two of us taking away their meal-ticket. Good point 'Enry, I thought, The Professor always has every angle covered. I tell ya this much … there ain't no flies on our 'Enry, he's as sharp as my missus's tongue when I've left the freezer door open.

A little while later we arrived at some gym. To be honest, it looked fackin' desolate, but then again so do most of these establishments. Anyway, the scenery don't matter, we're here to get a job done, and the kind of dough I've been offered when I hand over this geezer (and (or) the bit of scratch) is a no-brainer. You see, for me, there could be ten of the fuckers in there and if they want to try and come between me and the chance of my kids having a fantastic, all-expenses-paid Christmas, well, on their heads be it, 'cos I ain't taking no fackin' prisoners. Well, apart from one: ya know, the geezer who the Scotch Mob want to give a seeing to!

The Professor delicately eased himself up the grass verge and peered through the emulsion-paint spattered window (they had to be decorating). Then, he quickly informed me that there were three of them inside. First the perpetrator. 'Who's that?' I asked. 'For pity's sake, Norm,' The Professor snapped back in a stifled whisper. 'You know, the geezer who's nicked the bit of cash off of Braveheart!' 'Oh right!' I said. 'So why didn't you just say that then?' At which point The Professor shook his head, laughing. 'Right, once again,' The Professor said. 'There's the geezer we're after ... a little fella with a clipboard ... and a big juiced-up looking lump on a rowing machine.'

'Right!' I thought to myself, this is my field of expertise. So I tell 'Enry to hang fire until the geezer on the rower is fucked, then we can steam in quick style, your man can take the little geezer to the cleaners while I put Steve Redgrave to sleep and we bundle the wrong-un in the motor for a bit of lights in the boat-race (spotlight in the face) questioning. For once, 'Enry thought it was a great plan, and we swiftly put it into action.

The next few minutes were mayhem, as we charged through the door and went to work. I hit the big lump straight in the side of his head and he slumped fast asleep at the wheel … well, actually the oars. And that was that, we had it away: prize-fighter in hand, bagged, tagged and spitting and spluttering. Well, he was acting up so I winded him with a body shot and he was gasping for air. 'Enry told me to go easy, and we were off. We flew up the road like a bat out of hell, looking for a nice little quiet lane to do the questioning.

Well, at least that's what I thought we was going to do...

However, 'Enry had other ideas, and told me he was going to drive straight up the A1 and hand the package (meaning the perpetrator) over to the Scottish contingent. He said we'd do that, then we'd get weighed in (paid) and have it away on our toes, leaving them to deal with the safely delivered package.

Instantly the boxer geezer has gone all flaky and started begging us to take him to a house 'cos apparently that's where the bit of dough he's nicked is hidden. Well, my mate ain't called The Professor for nothing, 'cos 'Enry knew this would be the case from the off, and pre-empting this turn of events, was already driving the other way, back to South London.

A little while later we arrived; I took the boxer inside and then a few minutes later I walked back out with 40k (£40,000), oh, less a few hundred that he's already wasted down the bookies. Ya know what? It turns out I knew him. This fighter and I had worked together in Camden a few years earlier. Honestly, he was a nice geezer, in fact a lovely reliable geezer who had fallen by the wayside. Apparently, he'd got himself addicted to marching powder (cocaine) and it was fackin' his whole life up. He almost broke down when I told him that The Professor was going to put a good word in for him with his Guv'nor. Look, it's like this, we've all done wrong at one time or another, and I honestly didn't want to make this once-staunch geezer's life any worse. Oh, and secretly before we left, I dropped him a monkey (£500) and said, 'Sort yourself out me old mate, 'cos I'm telling you, it ain't worth the agg!' Our 'Enry never knew I done that. Sorry, Dad.

Me and Alfie were out one day on a bit of business, and we had a run-in with these blokes...

Anyway, one of the lunatics started giving it large, saying, 'You'd better watch your backs ... do you know who's backing us up?' So, Alfie asked, 'Well go on then, why don't you give us a clue?' Then one of them hollered, all confident, 'The Bucklands ... that's who! Norman and Alfie.' And with that, Alfie shouted back, 'Well go and fucking get them then. In fact, call Alfie Buckland now, and we can all wait here for him!' To which the geezer replied, 'Why, who the fuck are you then?' And Alfie replied, 'I AM ALFIE BLEEDING BUCKLAND, YOU IDIOT!' As you would expect, their faces dropped a foot, and they immediately fucked off down the road.

Matt Legg got in a spot of trouble one day in a local boozer. Apparently, he was out with his missus and slightly worse for wear when a bunch of geezers jumped him from behind. Matt being the fighter he is, immediately started to have a tear-up with them, but there were women and kids in the place screaming and he didn't want to frighten them and so he stopped. However, over the next few days it started getting to him and he went looking for them. He came across one of them in a shop up town and knocked him out cold, and I even think he took a samurai sword to one of the others to put the fear of God into him.

A few days later, one of these lunatics called me up and wanted to know if I could sort it out between them. I asked him how many of them were there and he said there was four or five of them. So, I said, 'Why the fuck did you try and take Matt on?' And he told me they were pissed up, and off their heads on coke. Oh, for fuck's sake I thought, this wasn't going to be easy. You see Matt is like a dog with a bone, and if someone has done him wrong, he seeks retribution, and it was obvious to me that he would bide his time and get his revenge one day. And he did…

Around this time, Matt had had enough of the shit and dropped everything and went off on a holiday to America. However, when he came back, he caught up with them all one by one. This wasn't the first time people had called me up to dampen a fire, as if I was some sort of godfather. I once had another call from a geezer saying, 'Norm, can you help us out? Matt's after us for money!' To which I replied, 'Right son, I'll give you a bit of advice … just pay the man up, 'cos I'll tell you this for nothing, you won't fackin' beat him!' These geezers were shitting themselves.

The story was this. Matt was doing a bit of debt collection work and he was on their case for the bit of dough they owed. Anyway, as I expected a few days later I found out that they had all paid up. Matt is a clever geezer and would always ask me for advice. And on many occasions, Matt and I have sat and talked over a whole load of issues. But Matt's a lot like me, and not one to have a fast-one pulled on him; he's a lovely friendly sort of geezer but don't ever take his kindness for weakness – 'cos you'll very soon regret it.

Oh, going back to working for Vic on them big concerts. I remember in particular one time very well, 'cos I had a little run-in with someone I actually did wish I had killed … yeah, and I mean that. 'Ere listen…

In the summer of 1997 we were working on that Wacko Jacko's (Michael Jackson) 'History' tour. This particular gig was over in Sheffield at the 'Don' something or other, and we were there as part of the merchandise minders. Like I've told you, the merchandise game was a nasty little business, with every little firm wanting the punters at the event buying their bit of clobber, and we were the heavies for Mr Bellamy, who were there to make sure that no fucker stepped on his toes. Well, as it turned out, on this occasion there was very little bother. Well except for one little incident that involved a well-known celebrity, Jimmy Savile. Fuck me, I don't like putting this evil little cunt on a pedestal, but at that time he was big news, and everybody loved the dirty cunt.

So, I was just having a walk about making sure no one was taking the piss, when I spotted this little fucker harassing the merchandise crew. Now, one of these young girls on the team was a bit of a model, and an up-and-coming actress as well; I won't mention her name 'cos she's big news these days. Anyway, she seemed to be handling the situation okay, and this young man, who I think was her boyfriend, looked like he had the situation under control, so I walked away and left them to it. But about half-hour later I was having another mooch about and spotted the same low-life cunt harassing the young girl again; only this time he had his hands all over her, and the boyfriend was being spoken to by this cunt's burly gorilla of a minder. Anyway, I'd seen enough so I steamed over to put the block on him. 'Oi, you dirty cunt,' I growled at the top of my voice. 'Put your hands back in their holster before I do you a bit of damage!' 'Now then my good man, do you know who I am?' he replied back all entitled, like he owned the place. 'Yes, I fackin' do, you low-life cunt! Now move away before I really lose me rag!' I glanced over and noticed the girl looked all worried, so I nodded my head and winked as if to say, step away, and she immediately moved a few paces back.

With that the cunt's gorilla stepped up, and I gave him an open-palm slap and almost took his head off. It didn't knock him out, but it was enough for him to keep out of my way. Then, I grabbed the scrawny little shell-suit-wearing wrong-un round the throat and whispered to him, saying, 'Look here you horrible little wrong-un, I know exactly who you are. I've never fackin' liked you, and you're starting to annoy me. Now, fuck off before I drag you up on that stage and show you up for the depraved little cunt you are!'

Well, as you would expect, he didn't hang about, and immediately, him and his minders had it away. A few months later I was doing a show around Christmastime and my pal said, ''Ere Norm, look who's over there. It's your best pal!' 'Now then – now then – now then!' I said, looked over, gave him a scowl and a growl, and he behaved like a choirboy for the rest of the night. With hindsight, I wish I'd have smashed the cunt to pieces when I had the chance, 'cos if I'd ripped off his winkle, he wouldn't have had the urge to molest all those innocent little kids, now would he? So, as the great crooner himself sang: *Regrets, I've had a few, but then again…*

I used to look after a geezer called Tony Ash; I was his right-hand man for a few years. Tony owned the top high street clothing retail outlets, Nickleby's and Copyrights. These places stocked designer Italian clobber, and Tony had loads of these lucrative retail outlets up and down the country. Anyway, apparently the security staff were up to no good, so he brought me in to keep an eye on them all; stuff was going missing, and Tony wanted to put a stop to it. So, I went in and worded the fackin' lot of 'em up: I told them that if any stock goes walkies, I would take it out of their wage-packets. They didn't like that, but knew they had to behave before I got the hump.

Tony was a capable geezer himself, he was a bouncer, a minder, debt collector – the lot. There wasn't much Tony hadn't been involved in. But as Tony said, it's always best to have a growler on the firm who these cunts won't dare try and mug off. You see, they'd taken Tony's kindness for weakness, and it just wasn't on. I mean, let's have it right, these geezers were getting 50 per cent discount off any of the high-end clobber (and I was in for the same slice of discount) so they had no excuses for half-inching it. So, I watched his stores up and down the UK and put a block on the thieving-handed security boys. I did a lot of work for Tony – he had his fingers in all sorts of tasty and profitable pies.

Tony ended up having a row with the big boxer geezer from Luton who I had taken to the cleaners in the ring a few years earlier. This boxer was a big name round Luton at the time, but he was a fackin' idiot, shouting his mouth off all over the place, trying to act like Al Capone. Anyway, he stepped on Tony's toes and Tony ended up giving him a good hiding.

You know as a minder you can get a call from anyone at any time. And with my name gaining respect, mainly down to all the shit I'd been through over the years, it was obvious to me that one day I'd get an even bigger call…

And I did, when one day this local millionaire geezer approached me with an offer I just couldn't refuse; well, if I'm honest, he bought me.

Look, I don't want to give out his name, 'cos he's a businessman, and initially he did help me out quite a bit. What he did was, he offered to pay off my ex-missus on the mortgage I had on two properties. You see she was into me for half of one of them, but I wanted to keep it, so with hardly a word said he slung in fifty-large (£50,000) for me to get shot of her. And it worked, she pocketed a nice bit of scratch, and I got my house back – perfect. Then, over the next few years I grafted my bollocks off doing all sorts of shit as a thank-you. Don't get me wrong, he put me on an earner too. But looking back at the 50k he threw me, in his eyes he probably thought he owned me.

So, I worked as his minder, but hang on don't get too excited. It wasn't quite like the glorified idea you're picturing in your head about the job of a minder, no. This was more along the lines of a Terry and Arthur kind of affair, as in the old TV comedy series, *Minder*. It was like a time and motions study: he checked the time, while I did all the bleeding motion. Look, it wasn't quite as bad as that. I mean yes, I minded him wherever he went, but I also got treated like a bit of a lackey – a bit of an errand boy. You know, a sort of, 'Do this, do that and I'll see you alright,' kind of thing. And let's just say, he liked a bit of a booze-up, and from two in the afternoon when he hit the bottle I'd have to be on the clock. But being the kind of geezer I am, I never moaned, I never got aggro, I just got on with whatever he threw my way. And fuck me, did he throw it...

Now, because of my name being well-known, the minder part of the job was okay. Although, he'd often go around town throwing his weight about, someone would have a pop at him, and I'd immediately get a phone call to go down and put the frighteners on the geezer in question. And now and then this would be an ex-employee of his. To be honest, I should've heard the alarm bells right there and then.

One time I got a call to go down to a little drinker I mentioned earlier called The Bell. Apparently, this geezer who had worked for this gaffer of mine before, was kicking off with him, things got a bit heavy and the ex-employee said he was going to have my gaffer's throat cut, and other unmentionable stuff that put the fear of God in him. Anyway, the geezer was bang on the money for having the needle with my gaffer, but he had to have a pull, 'cos whether or not I agreed with my gaffer was irrelevant; I was on the payroll and part of my job was to watch his back. So I packed up what I was doing and shot down The Bell.

When I arrived, my gaffer started shouting and hollering. He was like a kid in a school playground, pointing at the geezer, trying to manipulate the situation in the hope that I gave him a hiding. But I didn't need to lay a hand on him: he was shitting himself from the very first second he saw me walk in. Anyway, I told my governor to take a walk while I had a word and told the geezer to leave it there. I told him that he knows I'm his enemy's minder and that he couldn't just go around offering up threats 'cos I'd have to step in and really fall-out with him. Obviously, that was the last thing he wanted to happen, so he left a bit lively. Later that evening I went back to my governor and told him it was all under control and that the geezer was going to drop by and apologise. All sorted, then, bang, it was on to the next bit of agg. Which wasn't too far off, 'cos my governor was a proper wrong-un, this geezer could start an argument with fackin' Santa Claus.

Just to give you an idea of the sort of cash he has wrapped around him, I'll tell you what he's into. Right, he owns engineering plants that build the mechanical bits for the oil rigs, you know the bits that drill for the oil. Well, his business takes care of all of that. It's big fackin' business, and probably the reason he's rolling in it – the man's fackin' loaded. But he knows it and uses his wealth like power, to bully and manipulate people. He isn't the first to lord his dough about, and he certainly won't be the last. But this geezer's wallet and overblown entitlement makes him believe he can do as he wishes. Well it just ain't on, as many have told him.

He was having some trouble with a load of Gypsies who worked for him down the plant. Anyway, he'd sent this local hard nut down to sort it out, but they point-blank told him to fuck off and the big tough guy shat himself; these geezers were coming it strong and even the Old Bill had turned a blind eye. (I imagine they were on a wager for their silence as well!) So, he called me up and asked me to have a word. And as soon as I walked in the place these troublemakers began apologising; they knew of me and my reputation and didn't want it to get messy – which it would've done if they had not shut up, packed up, and fucked off down the fackin' road, and this is what I told them. And they left without a ruffled feather.

But like I say, I wasn't just a minder, my job was like Terry McCann's, in the TV series *Minder*; I was a minder who got his hands dirty around the place: the 'place' mostly being one of his big fackin' houses. Anyway, whether it was shovelling shit at one of his places, or round the yard at his workplace, humping great steel girders about, he'd have me at it, at it continuously, while all the time cocked-and-ready to down tools and go and sort out a bit of agg that he had caused. 'Ere listen, even when I came out of hospital and wasn't supposed to be working, he had me going at it, grafting like a twenty-year-old or Billy Whizz (the constantly running schoolboy in the comic *Beano*). I was fucked! To be honest, after I'd had a couple of heart attacks, I hoped he'd let me take it easy for a while until I got myself back on top form, healthy again.

But no, he's a fackin' wrong-un, he'd just go on and use and abuse me. Then shortly after that, he brought his old fella in on the firm, got himself a new bit of skirt to be his on-tap lackey, and swiftly made his excuses to stop my work and my pension.

15

THE WILD WEST: NO PLACE FOR A
COBBLE-FIGHTER

Writers' Note
When a new wave of muscle arrived, fists immediately took a back seat,
as guns, knives, and hefty lumps of bird (prison sentences) took centre
stage. This was never going to sit well with our protagonist – but he had
to survive, and as weapons were the order of the day, a cobble-fighter's
days began to slip away.

My dad, Alfie Snr, was a doorman. Dad worked his special,
albeit slightly questionable, magic all over the place. He'd
done The Grosvenor, The Crown, and many other places
all over Aylesbury. Dad was always head doorman with my
Uncle Chris playing the part as his equally well-equipped
second. Dad used to take me and my brother to work with
him, we were young then, just a couple of little ruffians,
scruffy little fuckers; angels with dirty faces, yet with brawn
and 'tasty fists' as our dad would say. And back in the day
Dad would stick us on the doors with great big fackin' dicky-
bows wrapped around our Gregorys; we must've looked
fackin' crazy. Anyway, due to Dad throwing us straight
in the deep end, by the age of fourteen we were full-on
working on the doors like men, as we grafted our way up

this apprenticeship, going full throttle, getting a quick-fire fighters' education, picking up tips and tricks as we waded in and fought.

It was at this very young age that I began to notice some right horrible cunts coming up for a bit of agg; all these types were trying to muscle their way in on a wing and a prayer, and I learned very quickly how to handle them. Dad had a funny way of going about things. If he put someone out of the premises and they started coming the Billy Big Bollocks, Dad would give them a smack and make them say sorry. He'd make them say it louder and louder, he'd make them plead until everyone in a 200-yard radius could hear them grovel. But as you know by now I adopted a different approach, and like I said earlier, I was a gentle, kind-natured sort of boy. However towards the end of my training, after receiving loads of abuse, I started to retaliate. We worked everywhere on the doors, from Hemel Hempstead, Wycombe, Bedford, Milton Keynes, Reading, Oxford – and tons of other bars, clubs and boozers up and down the country.

Another thing that instantly taught me a few lessons as a youngster was when I used to go to London with the travellers to the horse shows. I mixed with a lot of travellers and got to know their way of life really well. Like I've said before, I was never a bully, and this I think was something I picked up from the travelling community. But sometimes, no matter how nice I tried to be, trouble was just around the corner. If I'm brutally honest, I preferred frightening people with words and an almighty fackin' roar rather than hurting them physically, but sometimes words just weren't enough. Even as a young boy my mouth was as booming and loud as any geezer's who was twice my age: I think my spuds (balls) must've dropped when I was in the fackin' womb. Listen, I was never going to be a fackin' choirboy, my destiny was mapped out when I was nothing more than a glint in my dad's eye.

Lenny McLean was a big powerful bloke on the doors. A few people took a disliking to him, and I guess they disliked me to a certain extent as well. You see, door work can change you. A lot of people take the piss on the doors, and it gets you a bit irate and aggressive, there's no getting away from it, but it turns you into a bit of a horrible cunt at times, too.

People used to compare me to Lenny McLean: for instance there was the way I held myself on the door, my facial expressions, and the way I screamed used to turn people to jelly where they stood. You see, when you're going up against a few men you can put the fear of God into half of them just by waving your hands about as you growl at them. Plus, the fact that I would always seem to grow three times my actual size when I had the hump. And all of this artillery was perfect for when the odds were stacked against me, as they sometimes were. I was like a peacock raising its feathers, making your eyes pop out at the sheer sight of them. But listen, most of it was sheer bravado, it was all just for show. However, I realised very quickly that if this strange little show of extreme confidence and power worked, you hardly ever had to lay your hands on them and hurt them – so it was a win–win situation.

Talking about McLean for a minute. Yeah, he was one big, strong, powerful geezer, and I bumped into him a few times while working around Camden, Kentish Town and Hammersmith, etc. One night I was working for Star Guard Security, minding this geezer called Vic Bellamy at one of his client's concerts at Wembley Arena, where we had access to all areas. (Incidentally, this client was the rock star, Prince.) Anyway, the security boys started to give it the big one to me, so I gave them a good telling-off. The next night, knowing I would be there, the security firm brought McLean down to have a word. Now Lenny didn't speak to me, he just floated into the room like some gangster from yesteryear, stared, using that menacing eyebrow scowl of his, and addressed the whole room with some strange sort of animated intimidation. Now, that stare alone was enough to turn most men to stone, but it didn't work with me 'cos I was frightened of no man. I was doing the job I was getting paid for and nothing and nobody would ever change that. Mind you, the other geezers on the firm looked like they wanted to crawl up the nearest exhaust-pipe. Look, some geezers don't give a fuck, and some immediately get the wind up: I'm the former type.

At times it can be hard being a doorman, and for me it was a job I'd done my whole life, but I wouldn't bullshit you, it was fackin' hard, and sometimes it could be graft and arsehole every day. And where Lenny worked in the West End in places like the Hippodrome and the Camden Palace, he was known as one hard bastard and was very intimidating to look at. Lenny could win most of his fights with a simple look and, to be quite honest, I used that same kind of look a few times in various places myself, and, believe me, it worked a fucking treat. So, let's say I learnt from Lenny how to be the master. A geezer that to a lot of people was recognised as the cream of the crop. And yeah, on his plot, he was a man of worth was McLean.

I have been asked my opinion of Lenny many times over the years. I've met lots of people who said he bullied them; they said he intimidated them to get what he wanted. But was that bullying, or was it just business? Listen, when a certain firm want some contract done, they'll do whatever it takes to beat the rest of them to the finish line. So, perhaps that was all it was: perhaps he just saw his need was greater than theirs. Look, I don't know, and if I'm honest, I don't fackin' care. He was a name, a persona, and one hell of a character. And for the most part I thought he was a good geezer. So, I guess you'll just have to make up your own minds...

When I go to work in a club or pub I'm a gentleman but you have to change when it kicks off and you have to change a lot. And like with Lenny, it becomes an act, a character that you work on and dramatise. And back in the day, I found the louder I screamed the soberer troublemakers became. It put the fear into them, and in a great deal of the pubs I was by myself, and this little gem worked like magic. Fighting the average bloke on the street was easy, 'cos most of them were drunk and I could take my time with them. And sometimes I wouldn't even fight unless they were beating the fuck out of me, at which point all hell would break loose.

You see at times it wasn't about the punishment I could dish out: it was more about the punishment I could take. And with me, I could take the hidings and lap it up; I'd take a beating for a few minutes until *boom* the beast in me would be released and I'd do a number on them. Most fights would blow up and erupt and I'd be the man to finish them. But when I got older it was a lot easier to just knock them out sharpish; I'd save my stamina for later in case it really came on top.

One afternoon, around 1987, I popped into a boozer called The White Horse in Leverstock Green with a few of my mates. We were looking for work, hoping they needed some doormen. Anyway, the manager clocked us and informed us that a well-known face on the manor, Manny Clark (who was a good boxer) was running the place. The manager must have called Manny up on the phone, 'cos within a few minutes this Manny geezer turned up with a few of his hefty looking pals. He obviously had the hump, thinking that our little firm was trying to muscle in and take over his gaff: he didn't look fackin' happy.

As luck would have it, Manny and I hit it off immediately and simply saw it as an oversight. And as a result, Manny offered us all work. Manny ended up getting a contract for a nightclub in Buckinghamshire which was quite a rowdy old place. This club 'officially' shut its doors at two, but then the revellers were allowed to go upstairs, out of the way, to party for the rest of the evening. There were some right characters in there, and a load of rival firms from Chesham and Amersham used to frequent the place, and they'd be baying for each other's blood … they fackin' hated each other.

Now, due to the fact that I lived in the area, Manny asked if I'd go over and work the place. This was ideal for me as it was right on my manor. But what these clever little fuckers would do was come into the club in small numbers of three and four, then once inside they'd gather together as two big firms and meet up for an almighty fackin' tear-up. There they'd be in a stand-off, two rival gangs opposite each other, with menace building. Then with the atmosphere completely moody, they would run at each other like something out of the Wild fackin' West. They were a right load of lunatics.

On one occasion, Manny ran in and was smashing into them, throwing them at me as I was rushing them to the top of the stairs for the other doorman to take them from me and eject them onto the pavement. There was four of us working that night, and we were knocking them out and throwing them out in droves. Just as the fight started calming down, I heard the receptionist girl screaming at the bottom of the stairs. It turned out that another doorman, a man called Mad Ginger Callaghan, was throwing them out, and the receptionist was screaming in fright because Ginger was throwing them down the fackin' stairs. Even though they were battered and bruised, most of these fuckers would just walk off into the sunshine making their way from the club. These kinds of fights would occur week-in, week-out – it was raving fackin' lunacy.

Another night, this woman that Manny used to chat-up was walking through the club when Manny said, 'Alright sweetheart,' and pinched her on her bum. Now, Manny was only joking, but what he hadn't noticed was that the girl's boyfriend (who was also a boxer) was stood at the bar, clocked it, and ran across and banged Manny straight on the chin. With that, Manny smashed him on the jaw, and he went straight down. However, being a boxer, he bounced straight back up on his pins (legs) and decides he wants to go toe-to-toe with Manny. Anyway, me not being privy to the facts, I've run in and grabbed the geezer round the throat and immediately gone to throw him out, when Manny's started shouting at me, 'Don't throw him out, Norm ... he's alright!' So, I said: 'Yeah but I just saw him bang you on the fackin' chin, Manny!' And Manny replied adamantly, 'Yeah, that's right Norm ... but it was my own fackin' fault ... I only went and pinched his bird's arse without knowing she was with him.' Thankfully, the boxer geezer held out his hand to shake Manny's, and gracefully took the apology. And with that, all was forgiven and forgotten.

Another night, Manny had a run-in with this Scottish boxer they used to call Hamish MacTavish. Apparently, MacTavish's missus had kicked off over something, and in the mayhem, Manny ended up smashing Hamish proper, and knocked him on his arse. With that, I ran in like a fackin' derailed steam train, I grabbed the Jock (Scotsman) from the floor and dragged him all the way across the club to the main door to out him. The Jock was kicking off, saying he wanted to fight Manny. Manny shouted something over to him, like, 'Now listen here, I run the fackin' door in this club and I decide who leaves and who stays. You played up and got what you deserved.' The geezer was looking at me all confused, so because he was in no mood to let it go, I tried to put an end to it, by saying, 'Look, I know of a gym called Kennelly's. So, if you want to sort this out proper, you can have it out with him there, can't you?' Realising I had the situation in hand, Manny just walked off and left me to sort it. Anyway, a fight was arranged for the following Saturday. Manny had no need to sharpen himself up, 'cos he was always trained up and ready, so there was certainly no need for him to step-up the anti. But as we had first anticipated, the Jock never showed up anyway. Because, like most of them when they're boozed-up, fuelled-up and moody, they're all trap (mouth) and no arsehole!

Oh, let me tell you a bit more about the Kennellys in Hemel Hempstead. Right, the Kennellys were a family of boxers who owned fruit and veg stalls, and they kept these barrows stocked-up and going, from produce grown on their own land. Roy Kennelly had a boxing gym on his farm with punchbags, other equipment and a proper sized ring to spar and fight in. So, if me or Manny had a fight in the club and someone wanted to sort things out, we would do it the right way and organise a tear-up over at Kennelly's gym. Obviously, squaring it with the geezers beforehand. And we'd say to the wannabe boxers: how do you want it? Gloves on, or gloves off? It's up to you. Then once the fight was arranged, and the night was upon us, if Manny was stepping up, I'd referee for him, and vice versa. Strangely enough, most of the men we fought down at that gym Manny ended up employing.

Manny would always say to me on the door, 'Norm, you're always very calm … I very rarely see you lose your temper, and you're always smiling.' And this is the way I've always been. Still, when the roar has to come out and the beast has to be unleashed, out comes the other side of me. Then and only then, are all bets off, and at that point most people don't wanna know. But for the most part, I try to have a smile on my face and stay decent, calm and fair to everyone.

Manny is a few years younger than me, but as most of you will know, a few years age difference means nothing in the ring. Manny and I sparred back in the day when we were both amateur boxers, we had a good few little tear-ups. And then, a few years later the two of us boxed together on a few unlicensed shows, including one in Cambridgeshire. It was a good show promoted by Ricky English, staged in a big marquee next to a Gypsy camp.

Now, my mate Barry was a good pro boxer: he'd had about eighteen fights in his time. Barry fought the likes of Bobby Frankham, and he also sparred with some other top boys of the era, from Kirkland Lang and even Frank 'Know Wot I Mean 'Arry?' Bruno. We worked in many places together, places where many famous people would frequent. One particular gaff of this ilk that we looked after was a place called Friars. Bands and singers like the Rolling Stones, Adam Ant and many more used to come there, and if anything ever kicked off, everyone stuck together. People would call me outside shouting, 'Norm, we need you outside!' And as we got outside the troublemakers would jump on buses and you'd see us chasing them down the fackin' road. Barry was in court once, on a charge for 'supposedly' banging some geezer on the chin. Anyway, as a way of pleading his innocence, Barry stood in the dock and said, 'Look your grace, I'm a professional boxer. If I'd hit the so-called victim on the chin, he'd be in hospital!' Fuck knows how but somehow, he got off that one.

When I worked the doors, I got it into my head that I couldn't lose. You see, my motto was, if I lost, that would be it, 'cos I'd feel like I couldn't show my face on the doors ever again. It was a bit silly really, I mean, no one is invincible. Mind you, the only time I ever got a lot of trouble was when I was out of town, as people would come from everywhere and wouldn't know who you were. You see, in Buckinghamshire where I usually did the security, I'd usually be parked up on the pavement outside the venues and because they knew of my reputation, the aggro would be kept to a minimum.

I remember one night while working in Buckingham and I had my boy with me. He must've only been about fifteen years old at the time, so they had him collecting glasses at the venue. Anyway, these two brothers came in from Milton Keynes. I think they were karate fighting boys, and it appeared they'd seen a lamppost flyer saying I was The Guv'nor and that I'd fight any man on two legs. During the night my boy overheard them talking, so he came over to me and said, 'Dad, those men are setting you up. They are not drinking and saying that they're going to take you out!' So, I replied, 'Okay son, let them fucking try, eh boy!' Anyway, a little later on they went for it, so I gave one of them a slap while the other one took a chance and jumped on me from behind. My son spotted him, and he's done him instead. So there we were, me and my boy, back-to-back having a right tear-up with these cunts. Not long after this little episode I went away on Her Majesty's Pleasure for a spell. Then when I got released in 1997 I went straight back to work at that self-same venue I'd worked at before I got sent down. I kept my eyes peeled for the Karate Kids, but unfortunately, they never showed up for another bout of four against two. I liked this place with its ensuite casino. It was a good little number; they paid me well and I looked after them.

During the mid to late 1980s I worked a place called WKD in Camden's Kentish Town. This venue had been having a lot of trouble and the doorman had been smashed to pieces, and subsequently I was hired to go in there and sort the gaff out. You see, back then owing to my rep (reputation) if there was any trouble in these sorts of bars, they would quickly get me in to make the place sweeter for the good people that frequented them. So, I've walked in there with my usual animated confidence and muscle, with an added bit of bravado for good measure, I've stretched out my chest and sat alone at the end of the bar...

Now, my family the Bucklands were born out of Kentish Town and are well known and respected in the area. My uncle Perry Buckland had done a life sentence but kept his hands clean and his mouth shut and managed to see it through till he was gifted his Jam Roll (parole). Unfortunately, though, for whatever reason after his release, he sadly took his own life. But anyway, back to the story. As I was sat there minding my own business, this big firm of well-known drug dealers came over and started talking to me, at which point I started thinking to myself, I'm going to get murdered here, as one of them said, ''Ere, we don't like foreigners turning up on our manor!' And I replied, 'Well actually my old mate, this is my manor too,' and I quickly began to explain a bit about the Buckland family. Thankfully, they had heard all the stories passed down about my family and said, 'Listen, you're alright you are, Norm. It's outsiders we don't like on our patch.' I got on alright with them all in the end, and it turned out it was some of the other doormen they had a beef with. Looking back, it was a good job they knew of my family, otherwise I probably wouldn't have stood a chance on me Jack Jones (on my own). Still, I would've hurt a few of them in the battle, and they knew it.

When they were at their peak, I looked after that group Bros, at a gig at the Birmingham NEC. This was the same year they'd had that single out: 'When Will I Be Famous' or something, I think it was called. Now, these boys knew exactly who I was, because ten years before this we'd looked after them at a concert in Hemel Hempstead and they had asked us to carry their bags, and I said, 'Listen boys, we ain't no fackin' skivvies ... now liven yourselves up and carry your own fackin' gear!' Honestly, I didn't have a fackin' clue who they were, and to be honest, I didn't give two fucks. We done loads of up-and-coming bands in those days, bands and artists like: The Damned, Bow-Wow-Wow, David Bowie, Big Country, Eric Clapton. At some stage or another I've worked with the whole lot of them.

I'll tell you what, when people say you have to be careful who it is you're talking to, or perhaps in my case, who you might be about to give a dig to, well, they ain't fackin' wrong. I was working in this one place called WKD in Camden Town and one of the members of this well-known gangland family came in, acted the cunt, and I threw him out on his ear. This geezer (whoever he was) was only a youngster at the time, I never had a clue who he was, but I was just doing my job. Anyway, this man turned to me and said, 'Do you know who that is, Norm?' And I said quite abruptly, 'No, I don't give a fuck who he was!' A little later someone told me who his Clerkenwell family were, at which point I thought, oh for fuck's sake, me and my big fackin' trap! However, then I thought about it again and thought, if they turn up, I'll just tell them the truth, talk to them nicely, and hopefully they won't blow my fackin' head off. Fortunately, nothing ever came of it.

Tony Ash had got me a gig up North, I can't remember the name of the singer, but I was told to look after this man in a wheelchair. Anyway, after speaking to him for a while, it turned out he was the rapper's fackin' dad. If I'm honest, I never knew half the stars I was minding, 'cos they were up-and-comers, just starting out, and all a bit different to the likes of Harry Webb, or Cliff Richard to you lot who don't know him personally like what I do. ('Ere, don't take offence ... I'm only pulling your chain while I was trying to act all important and a bit posh.) But, joking apart, over the years I've minded all the big players, all the top superstars, from Bruce Springsteen to the king of blues himself, Eric Clapton.

Another time, I got a job on a Breast Cancer Awareness Day up in London. This was a proper professional event:

a red-carpet affair and all the bollocks that goes with it. It was full to the rafters with celebrities from all over the globe. I was working with my mate Daz at the time, but we got separated and he was put on the disabled entrance on his own for six hours. So, there I was chatting away to all these celebrities, and all the time giving Daz a piss-taking little wave every now and again, laughing my head off. Fuck me we had some laughs.

Mind you it wasn't all that jovial, because later that evening I got in an argument with some foreign taxi driver, and all his fackin' mates started jumping out of their cars with bats and other tools to set upon me. Suddenly, I've ended up on top of the ringleader cunt and I've seen red because of his attitude and bit half his face off; he ended up having forty-nine stitches for his trouble.

Back then when this sort of shit went down the 'beast' in me, as I used to call it, would just take over and I'd bite off anything in view; well, not anything ya saucy cunts, but you get my drift. I was a raving lunatic, I mean, back then I wasn't just trying to hurt them, I was trying to fackin' kill them – I was out of control. Then, once the fight was done, I would just walk off and go to some party as if I'd just been out for dinner. Mind you, the next day I'd be at work and couldn't even push the fackin' wheelbarrow; the pain would kick in and I'd end up in hospital from the hits I'd taken from the bats the night before.

I was sent in to straighten out one venue 'cos apparently they were having a bit of trouble with some local lads. Anyway, I shot in there and sorted out the grief and everyone was happy. Mind you I might have been a bit hasty, because shortly after that I started having a few problems with the owner over money. So, one night I steamed in there tooled-up with an axe and chopped his fackin' bar to bits – hey, it wasn't my fault, I thought I overheard him say he was desperate for some firewood for the cooking stove! Funny thing was, a little while later I was talking to this carpenter, and he was telling me he was working on some boozer and was struggling to get the axe marks out of the bar. Fackin' hell, what a turn up! But that was how my brain was back then, it was normal to me, nothing special. Looking back though, thinking about it, acting like that was probably a bit stupid, and it was a shame that the beef with the landlord got out of hand.

I was working in this one place called Directors over in Milton Keynes, and these four men were in there and acting up. Now, all of these fellas had big reputations and were known as right lunatics. On paper, I would have my work cut out taking one of them on never mind all fackin' four of them. These fuckers seemed to be finding their feet, but they were aware of my rep as well. As the weeks passed by, they were getting worse and there was nothing else I could have done, as it wasn't my door. They were causing trouble, fighting with everybody, and generally taking the piss. I knew I could take a good hiding and at the end of the day I had kids to feed and if I lost a fight, I also lost my pride, which wasn't going to happen.

Another time I was working upstairs in this place called Flames and it went off big time. There was a few of them there, then this one lunatic smashed me full-force in the head and broke his fackin' hand. 'Ere I ain't one to bullshit though, and I'll admit it did fackin' hurt me a bit. Although, it seems it didn't hurt me as much as it hurt the geezer with the broken hand – apparently, he was in agony. Anyway, it turned into a right fackin' tear-up, and one of the cheeky cunts even had the brass neck to gas me, that is spray me in the face with tear gas. Now, fortunately for me, I had been gassed a few times by my brother Alfie. Yeah, you heard it right, my own fackin' brother gassed me. But eh, according to him it was just for a bit of fackin' fun.

I remember I was on the toilet and the door flung open and there stood my brother, can-in-hand gassing the fuck out of me. And, while I was in extreme pain, he was just stood there laughing his head off saying, 'Just ignore it, Norm. Don't breathe in deep and keep your eyes wide open!' Now, I don't know if Alfie had had some Romany premonition about this happening to me some time in the future and thought he would get me prepared, or if he was just a wicked fucker who was having a laugh at my expense. But whatever the truth, this preparation worked, because, years later I was in a tear-up with a bunch of fuckers who thought they could beat me by gassing me first. Then seconds later, they were slumped there bleeding all over the place, and I was still standing without a mark on me, they never had a clue what's just happened. Now that's what I call fighting against the odds. It was just the way I was made. I could take a fackin' good beating, even a fackin' gassing, and I'd still be standing there bold as brass. I could take all the pain they dished out to me, then I would rear up all cranky, they'd take one look at me and think fuck that and have it away on their toes.

I was in this garage one day filling my motor up with juice when I clocked some youngsters who I'd had a run in with down some club I was minding. These were dangerous little fuckers and didn't give a fuck for nobody. Anyway, seconds after they spotted me, they jumped out of their motor and gassed me. The gas didn't bother me one bit, 'cos I'd been gassed a few times before. So, I just kept fighting them in the middle of this garage like a lunatic. With that, they must've got the wind up and dispersed a bit lively. I don't know what the fuck it is with me and gas, 'cos as I told you, my own brother had done it to me years earlier too and he reckoned he did it to get me prepared for the big bad world, saying that if ever it happens in the future, on the street, I'd be prepared for it. Fackin' hell, I should've belted him with a chopper and said, 'Oops, sorry bruv … I was just getting you prepared, just in case you…'

I was working in one place in South London on the doors. This was a proper rough place where previously we had thrown six geezers out and they returned to iron us out with baseball bats. This lot instantly set upon me and were smashing lumps out of me; it must have lasted for about half an hour. The bats were actually breaking, and my jaw was broken on both sides. Fortunately, I managed to overpower them and smashed every last one that had the balls to stick around. After that fight I had to have my whole jaw wired and rebuilt, not for the last time. It was bad, there was blood spurting out all over the gaff, and I could hardly speak a word for weeks. This was fackin' horrible for me, 'cos I don't half like to rabbit.

Shortly after this little row, my mate gave me some tear gas and I'm not ashamed to say that after that experience I carried it with me every day. 'Cos looking back at the situation if I hadn't had my wits about me, I could have easily died – better be prepared next time, Guv. After my pal gave me the tear gas, he asked if he should try it out on me. So, I was on the toilet in one of our clubs when the door gets kicked off its hinges and the fucker ran in and sprayed me right in the fackin' face; this was the first time I'd been totally bolloxed in my entire life, and this fucker just stood there laughing like some psycho. I learnt after that that if I ever got gassed again, I would try not to panic and just breathe slowly, just as my brother Alfie had told me.

I also got tear-gassed straight in the mouth by a bunch of geezers and was just on my way to get a 12-bore shotgun out of my car when the Old Bill arrived. My plan was just to scare these youngsters, I was going to shoot over the tops of their heads and scare them. But the Plod (the police) hung around too long and fackin' ruined my plan. I had big blisters all over my mouth from the gas and was a bit sore too. Then, at the end of night, this big bird came down and tried kissing me on the fackin' lips, my mouth was so sore, I nearly had to pick her up and hold her above my head to stop her. In the end, during the mayhem, the soppy girl got a bit of payback when she managed to tear gas herself – daft cow. Mind you, it's quite funny now, looking back on it.

I was once gassed by a bunch of geezers over in Brixton. But unbeknown to them by that point in my life I'd sort of started to get used to the effects of gas, and even though it nearly fackin' blinded me, I kept on fighting. My jaw was broken again, and I ended up in hospital, again. My jaw was hanging off my fackin' face. What happened was this. A big gang of lunatics had kicked off and they grabbed my pal Ginger and ripped his shirt and chain off. Now, as you will know by now, no matter what the odds are, I would never leave a pal down on the deck, and with that reasoning I rushed over to help him. And that was when it happened … SMASH … I took a dig from the side – they'd done me in the jaw. And to add insult to injury the cunts gassed me. This canister went off like a fire extinguisher, and everyone fucked off out the way of it. Unfortunately, this was the moment when I steamed in and got caught with a cheeky belt to the chops for my trouble. My jaw exploded: it was smashed to pieces in three places. Anyway, I put that little experience down to another bad day at the office.

16

HALF-TON PRIZE FIGHTER

Writers' Note
Our man would never back down from a challenge: it didn't matter who, what, or even where it came from! It could have been a mountain lion … he wouldn't have cared. You see, Stormin' Norman would have had a roll-around with it, anytime!

'Who's the Fackin' Guv'nor?'

Fackin' hell, I get sick of hearing this argument up and down the country. Listen, no one owns the title, and no one can lay claim to it, but if you've earned it yourself and it's the name you're known for, then it's something you keep, and I'll never surrender the right to call myself it … I'm The Guv'nor, and that's just the way it is.

Look, being The Guv'nor ain't about winning some belt. It ain't about some honour you've earned in the ring, it's about what's inside of you … it's about that thing that beats in your chest, that thing inside you that's keeping you alive, and that's what being The Guv'nor was all about … keeping myself alive; staying on top by winning at any cost; on the streets, in whichever way I saw fit, and by whatever means were at my disposal.

I mean, c'mon, my great-great-grandfather was a Guv'nor; a fist-fighting man of honour, who was respected, feared, and revered in equal measure, and for all the right reasons. Not for bullying fear into people. No, his respect was earned just for being a tasty geezer with his fists! And that right there stayed with him long after he was dead and buried, and the lineage to this he left on the streets, and it quickly became a part of me. It was in my blood, and I had no way of containing it. And for that reason, Gypsy Jack Cooper will live forever, and from my descendants to theirs, it will echo through the passages of time. I'm The Guv'nor … and don't you forget it!

Listen, I'll never back down from a challenge: doesn't matter who, what, or even where it comes from! It could be a mountain lion … it doesn't matter, I'll have a roll-around with it, anytime!

When I was approached by young Joey Pyle (son of the legendary Joey Pyle Senior; the man who kicked off the whole unlicensed [unaffiliated] boxing game back in the mid 1970s) and his partner Ricky English, to offer myself up for some new era Guv'nor title, I fackin' jumped at the chance. Now, most people (like my brother) who know me of old, know that I didn't need to prove myself to anybody; I was The Guv'nor long before I decided to team up with these geezers, and that says it all. But listen, for me, I honestly believed that having my name up there with the likes of Lenny 'Boy' McLean and Roy 'Pretty Boy' Shaw was certainly something that would give my ego a boost; not to mention the kudos I'd gain as a result. In my eyes, as the youngsters say, it was a 'no-brainer'. So, I said, let's do it, boys! Let's get the wheels in motion...

These boys weren't new to the game, it was like walking and talking to these fellas; these fellas had put as many 'Z-list' unlicensed shows on, as Eddie Hearn and his old man had put on A-list ones, and, because of this, I was quite happy to throw my name into the mix.

Now, let's get one thing straight from the off. Look, I wasn't a young man, I was in my late forties for fuck's sake! But as I said earlier, I back down from nothing, and no challenge is greater than the will I possess to prove my worth. So, young Joe and Ricky took care of all the backroom business: they found the opponents, the venues and sold the tickets. Then I simply got ready to do the business with the gloves on.

Oh, just before I forget, one of my main sparring partners for those Mean Machine fights was my son, Buster: my boy could hold his own against me in the ring from a very young age. I'm guessing he must've only been about fourteen, but he was fit and strong, and just like his dad, didn't give two fucks for no one. Listen, most of us old-time guvnors could have a bit of trouble faced with a youngster like my boy, whether it be sparring or perhaps even on the cobbles. Look, like I said, I was way past my best, and I don't give a fuck admitting it. The only difference I could see is that geezers like me can take one hell of a hiding and we can keep on pushing forward using the old tricks we've learned over a great many years.

My first fight, and my debut for Mean Machine Promotions, was for the EBF Super Heavyweight British title against a man called JJ. The night of the big fight came, and as I'd expected, the venue was packed to the rafters. This was going to be a fackin' cracker, and the crowd were making themselves known as they waited on tenterhooks for the main event.

My opponent JJ visited me in the changing room before the fight, and asked, 'Eh, Norm, if I go down during the fight, you're not going to jump all over my head, are you?' And I said, 'Listen, if I think you're taking a fackin' dive; if I get the slightest idea, you're doing a Ronaldo, diving, and making a fackin' show of yourself, then yeah, I will stamp all over your fucking head ... 'cos I ain't being mugged off by no cunt!' JJ's line of enquiry made it clear to me that he was shitting himself before we even touched gloves.

Fight time...

JJ was already in the ring; he was in his corner waiting for me. This three-round fight was for the new EBF Guv'nor belt, although the belt wasn't ready on time, the boys at Mean Machine had planned to hand it over to the winner at a later date. Anyway, to me, this wasn't about some belt, this was more about following in the footsteps of the past Guv'nors like Roy Shaw and Lenny McLean: Guv'nors I succeeded to get where I am now.

Suddenly, the curtain at the back of the venue opened, and the lights hit me and revealed a scene that looked like something from a rock concert. The flashes were going off like some red-carpet event, and the crowd were buzzing and baying for blood. This place was filled with punters that were right up for a showdown, and believe me, there were a lot of haters in there that night: loads of the fuckers waiting for me to drop a bollock and lose. I was dressed in this big red robe and acting up for the crowd with all of my usual scowls and growls. This is all just bravado really, but it looks good, and as you know by now, I'm actually just playing a part, and the punters fackin' love it. All the usual motley crew were in attendance, but my lot were shouting louder than any of the haters; my boys were overpowering the place with their chants, and all you could hear was people screaming my name. (If you have access to a computer, you can still watch the actual footage on YouTube if you search my name.)

So as to not leave them disappointed, I screamed an almighty, 'WHO'S – THE – FACKIN' – GUV-NAAA!' While all the time doing muscle poses and screaming at them all. You see, one thing they get with me is one hell of a show. I never hold back, and I give them what they've paid good money to see. Anyway, the next thing you know, a gigantic spotlight like the ones you see in the big theatres shone right in our faces and I began pumping the air and spitting and hollering. I'll tell you what, the fackin' crowd there that night was fackin' hostile, and it was clear to see they were bang up for a row. Some of the security geezers were trying to hold us back, away from all the baying punters as they shouted stuff at us. It was obvious they were trying to aggravate me, in the hope that I kicked off like a lunatic. As we approached the stage, young Joey Pyle came over, so I grabbed hold of him and lifted him clean off the floor. At this point my adrenaline was through the roof, and I couldn't wait to get in the ring and unleash it on my opponent.

I began to amble my way down to the ring; while I was walking down a set of steps, fans were patting me on the back, hugging me and wishing me well. When I got to the ring, I glanced over at my opponent JJ, who was standing in his corner waiting for the show to begin, when suddenly, I saw red and tried to attack him through the fackin' ropes. JJ moved himself away from my grasp and his team looked on, wondering what I was going to do next. I hadn't even got in the ring yet and I was already trying to do him some damage, performing like a raving lunatic for all to see. Then the referee appeared out of nowhere and began pushing me away. I continued the bravado, walking round the ring and playing up to the crowd as before. Then, immediately, as I stepped onto the canvas, I unleashed a flurry of punches, while screaming and snarling at everybody around.

The MC for the event announced my opponent's name as he should, but then announced me as, simply 'Norman'! Cheeky cunt! I thought he would have at least ramped it up a bit and announced me as Stormin' Norman! I began to take my robe off, and the crowd screamed through the ropes. Now, as I was glaring over into the crowd, I spotted some bald geezer standing up in front of the ring calling me all the fat cunts under the sun. Fuck me, I remember thinking to myself, I've lost two stone for this fight – what a cheeky cunt! Anyway, I was there to put on a show, and so immediately I ran across the ring and began kicking the shit out of the rope, right where this troublemaker was stood, and in my mind, all I was thinking about was how I could turn his taunts into a future challenge. At which point I thought to myself, 'Right Guv, let's light this fucker up,' in the hope of fuelling a challenge. Apparently, this geezer had been kicking off earlier in the evening, so unbeknown to him, he'd already lined himself up for a telling-off.

Well, the taunts were coming thick and fast, so I jumped through the ropes and tried booting him in the head. Fortunately for me I still had hold of the ropes, 'cos with my leg kicking out I felt myself slipping and ready to fall arse-over-tit. Looking back at it now, I could easily have landed in a heap and made a right fackin' show of myself. Fortunately enough, I managed to keep my balance and landed perfectly on the floor, as I gripped tightly to my fackin' dignity. Then, now fully stable, I ran over to where the mouthy geezer was and grabbed him round the throat, pushing him back with a bit of force just to show him who was boss, and with that he fell down on the deck and I smashed him with a straight right shot. Suddenly, the place went nuts, and geezers began taunting one another while throwing punches and sticking the nut in all over the place; these fackin' idiots were even smashing shots into their own. Immediately, I was swiftly pulled from the mayhem and people were screaming for me to get back in the ring. Seeing sense, I climbed back up to the ring and made my way over to my corner and continued to watch the lunacy unfold.

By this point it was going nuts; in the first few rows on the outer perimeter of the ring people were standing on tables, throwing head-butts and all sorts of stuff. At which point, the announcer geezer (having seen enough) started shouting orders at the room to stop: warning them that if they didn't calm down, the whole show would be cancelled. Obviously, some of them didn't take a blind bit of notice, and the bald fackin' geezer who I'd knocked to the ground was still making threats and challenges at me from outside the ring. All through the mayhem, my great pal Matt Legg (the mediator) was right in the thick of it, trying to sort it out and calm everybody down; there were other people trying to do the same, but Matt is that fackin' big he stands out in a crowd. At this point, I was also shouting at people, telling them to calm down. That was until the reality hit me like a hammer, as I said to myself: Norm ... it was you who started it in the first fackin' place!

Well, it took a bit of work (mainly by Matt) and a few bust noses to calm it all down, and the fight was finally allowed to continue, and immediately got underway. Still feeling a bit aggravated, I ran out of my blocks, and headed straight for JJ like a bull in a china shop and instantly began smashing right and left shots into his body, as hard and as fast as I could. I must say, he was covering himself up quite well, and he also threw a couple of nice hooks back at me to counter. Suddenly, he caught me with a right nice shot smack bang on my temple. Mind you, it didn't shake me too much 'cos I was too busy getting in amongst it myself, as I bashed him with uppercuts and more hooks in an attempt to break him down. Suddenly, I caught him straight in the fackin' bollocks and he dropped to the canvas like a bag of soggy cement. With that, the referee ran across the ring to stop any aftermath, but I was still a bit wired and pushed him flying back from where he came. The ring announcer started his count, and as soon as they reached nine, young Joe jumped in the ring, happy as Larry and started hugging me. My opponent JJ didn't make the ten count and that was that: I was the new champion.

...*Now I'm The Guv'nor.*

It was all over; my fans were going absolutely nuts. Unfortunately, some geezers started arguing in the crowd again but I was oblivious to it. I was too busy screaming: 'WHO'S ... THE ... FACKIN' ... GUV-A-NAAA?' While my fans (the ones that weren't in a tear-up) stood cheering and beckoning to me, as they chanted along to my anthemic roars. I continued singing, 'I'm the fackin' Guv'nor,' and everyone began cheering and chanting my name: 'Norman – Norman – Norman...' they sang. And as they cheered, I stepped out of the ring, headed over to the bald geezer who seemed to have the right hump with me, and yelled, menacingly: 'YOU'RE – FACKIN' – NEXT – SON!'

A few minutes later and I'm backstage getting myself changed and having a bit of a relax, when Liam Galvin (the prolific YouTuber and film-man) came in to interview me. Next thing you know, my name was being called again, and it was young Joey Pyle, the promoter, making his way through

THE NEW GUV'NOR

the many well-wishers. And due to the fact that I felt bad for kicking the riot off in the first fackin' place, I immediately made my apologies to him. However, Joe was having none of it, and just walked over to me, laughing, and said the event went fucking perfect, and was exactly what he'd expected. But I still felt a little guilty, and went on to explain that the bald geezer in the crowd had been taunting me like a lunatic, calling me a fat bastard etc. Joey and I went over the whys and wherefores, and then had a good laugh about the whole fiasco.

To be honest, I still wasn't happy with myself; it was only meant to be a bit of bravado to get the venue pumping, and I felt as though I'd started a full-on fackin' riot. But Joe explained that you always get fights in the crowd and it's something that echoes back to the old unlicensed boxing days – he said it's par for the course Norm, no dramas.

Joe and Ricky English were nice about it and told me not to worry and said it would all be forgotten by the next morning. It was good of them to say all of this, and it made me feel a little better about what I saw as the unavoidable part I had played in it. Nevertheless, in my opinion I had set a bad example for the kids and women who were there taking it all in.

A few seconds later my opponent came in, saying he wanted to come and see me to clear the air before he left the venue. Anyway, I gave him a big Guv'nor hug, and we laughed it all off. JJ went on to explain that he knew it was all just playing up for the camera and the crowd – and knew there was no bad feeling whatsoever. He's a nice geezer, is JJ, he's a proper gent, and we remain friends to this day.

My uncle, Danny Butler, was at the fight, and he came in to see me and said that he had heard the bald geezer saying he wanted to fight me, and apparently he went over and offered him five thousand notes to make it happen. Strangely enough he declined. A little while later I spoke to the man of the moment. It turned out that he was a really nice geezer who just got carried away with the bravado of the night.

My next fight for Mean Machine was in a large marquee in Cambridge, where I fought a man called Dolph. Dolph was a giant of a man, yet he had a gentle nature to match his size. As you would expect, I applied some of my usual ringside antics, well look, it puts bums on seats, doesn't it? But all the bravado aside I stepped through the ropes, and fackin' hell I noticed straight away that he was a big cunt; he had arms like Arnie (Arnold Schwarzenegger) in his *Pumping Iron* days, plus, he was at least a foot taller than me. But as is my way, I never let it put me off: he's got a pair of fists and a set of ribs just like I have. So, that was that, I stuck my head down and went at him like a bull in a quaint little English ceramics shop. Listen, I ain't saying that far off eastern country's name, 'cos they've pissed me right off forcing us all into this poxy lockdown thing!

Anyway, there I was, smashing into his belly and ribs at the same time, lapping up his smashes to my head – it's hard to feel pain when your head's down and you're going to work yourself. Mind you, that being said, he did catch me with a hammer shot to my temple which fackin' dazed me for a minute – so much so, I heard ringing and was seeing fackin' stars, and not the stars you wanna be seeing. I very quickly got my head back in the room and went back to smashing at his ribs. But his arms were so big, they were covering the parts that, had I hit them, would easily have seen him hit the canvas. Right, I thought to myself, time for a bit of unlicensed villainy, as I hit him a little bit low and caught him right at the bottom of his belly. That's done him, I thought, as he toppled like a spent horse on Derby Day. The ref stepped in and TKO'd him (Technical Knockout) out of the game. And to be honest, I was happy he fackin' did, 'cos that was the hardest two minutes' work I'd had to do in a long time. Anyway, I walked straight over to the man and told him that he'd hurt me with the temple shot. We exchanged a few words of mutual respect, and the pair of us left the ring as friends.

A little while after that, Dolph came into my dressing room and we had a nice chat. He told me that all my ducking and diving had made it too difficult for him to lay a glove on me, and he also said I was too powerful and that he'd never been hit so hard, which was nice, because he had fought and sparred with some top-flight boxers in his time. He was a lovely man, and I hope he's still going strong and enjoying early retirement like I am.

A few months later, still in 2009, Joey put another show on at Caesars in Streatham. For some reason, my opponent didn't turn up to fight, but the belt from my previous title fight had arrived and was ready to be presented to me. The MC (Ricky English) asked Roy Shaw to come up to the ring and present me with it. So, let's get the facts of this in print.

Ricky began announcing to the crowd that this was the old Guv'nor passing his belt down to the new Guv'nor: that being yours-truly. He then went on to say, this is the old champ, Roy Shaw, passing it on to the new champ, and the whole crowd chanted and cheered, as this was the belt I should have been presented with at the JJ fight. A minute or two later, my name was called, and I jumped over the front seats and made my way to the ring.

I was dressed up to the nines with all my Tom and finery, looking every inch the part. I climbed through the ropes and immediately gave Roy a hug as the trigger-happy picture takers caught the moment for posterity. Then, as is usually the case with me, bang! I was hit with an almighty adrenaline rush and instantly began shouting, 'Who's the fackin' Guv'nor?' Roy held the belt up and I lifted him clean off the canvas, swinging him round shouting, 'This geezer's the real fackin' Guv'nor!' as a show of my ultimate respect.

Still holding Roy up, I began screaming at the top of my voice, rock and roll: 'Who's the fackin' Guv'nor?' You see, having watched all the videos of Roy over the years, I had massive respect for the geezer: this man was like a god to me and an ultimate Guv'nor and a force to be reckoned with on the cobbles. In addition, you have Lenny McLean, he was another legend and Guv'nor on the cobbles as well. So, let's just say, I was in good fackin' company, and was extremely proud to be following in these geezers' footsteps. This moment was an honour to hold in my fighting life journey and being passed the title by the Guv'nor of yesteryear was the icing on the cake; not to mention, an accolade that can never be taken away from me.

A few months later I defended my title against another big lump and well-known face on the scene called Steve Yorath. The bell sounded and I went straight at him, hitting him with body punches. He was an old pro, so he covered up well, and was counter-punching now and again, catching me to the head. I kept at him, then put him down after a left hook to the stomach. But being an old pro, he was back up at the count of eight and put his hand out all friendly like, to touch gloves. However, as I reached out to touch gloves the fucker threw a big right hand at my head, but luckily I managed to duck underneath it. We then smashed each other with a few heavy punches before I caught him with a right-hook that dropped him to the canvas again. Fortunately enough for him, the bell saved him once again, and moments later we were back at it and into the next round. I tell you what, this man knew some fackin' tricks, which was obvious, given the fact that he'd been around the block a few times. At this point a few head-butts have gone in from both of us! (Well, at the end of the day, it was unlicensed.) Anyway, as the rounds were going on I was getting more knackered by the second. Fortunately, as we came out for the third and final round, I caught him with a few shots, followed up with an uppercut and he was on his knees and failed to make the ten-count. This made me the winner, and was the first and unfortunately last, title defence I was fit enough to take on.

So, that was that. It was all over, and I went over and gave him a big hug, but once again, it was kicking off in the crowd, so I started shouting at people not to fight and spoil the night. To be brutally honest, I wished I'd been a bit sharper for the fight, 'cos Steve was an old pro and was extremely well versed in a boxing ring. Coincidentally, if you have a look on YouTube, you can see Steve not only fighting, but refereeing a few of these unlicensed fights on similar shows.

The thing you need to remember is, at this point I was almost fifty years old, and fighting young geezers in their prime. Most of these boys were under thirty years of age, and like me back in the day, they were champing at the bit to get a result, these geezers were hungry and ready to lay their lives on the line. But me, fackin' hell I was well past my best: I was close to spitting out my gumshield and calling it a day. I was in preparation to move on to bigger and better things – I'd done all I wanted to do, and had had enough of the fight game.

It was at around this time that Joey Pyle announced that he wanted me to take a dive in a fight at a packed venue against Dave Courtney. It was obvious to everyone around that Joey just didn't give a fuck; he knew it would be packed to the rafters and lining his pockets with dough was the only thing in his fackin' brainbox. Anyway, I told them to fuck off, saying I would fight him in a proper bout but wouldn't roll over for no cunt. Apparently, when asked, Dave said: 'I'm not fighting Norman Buckland … what do you think I am, fucking suicidal?' Although, he followed the comment up by saying that his mate the notorious Charlie Bronson would step up to the plate and fight me when he got out of prison. Now, for Dave Courtney this was the perfect get-out: it was obvious this would never happen, but it did Dave a side-stepping favour – Dave ain't fackin' silly.

People began broadcasting that Bronson was soon to be released, and if that was the case, I would have fought him no problem. I didn't really give a fuck. But Joey basically wanted me to sing to his tune and be some homemade puppet Guv'nor; someone they could pull the strings of and completely control. But I would never be that geezer; I never let anyone take me for a fackin' mug, and I never fackin' will.

Listen, in my heart of hearts I could have dealt with almost anyone, even after having two heart attacks and a fackin' stroke, I still would've taken the risk. And this was a fact that was proven in the Romany tea leaves and cards, when they told me I would always be The Guv'nor. They also told me that at this stage in my life I should only take three fights on, and according to my family heritage, when you take advice from the tea leaves, you have to listen to it, 'cos they believe it's the spirits who are sending the messages to these people.

Being The Guv'nor, I was asked to go down and show my face at some blue-collar event down London. So there I was, suited and booted and ready for the show, but halfway through I had to go to the toilet. Then when I was on my way back into the hall I started chatting to this geezer, when (through this open glass door) I spotted the MC for the event calling loads of well-respected men's names out and they were standing up, waving, and people were cheering and clapping. Then a few 'faces' stood up: Joey Pyle Senior, Roy Shaw, Charlie Breaker, Tony Lambrianou, and a bunch of other well-known gangster types. Suddenly, I heard the geezer say: 'And the man with the most colourful suit tonight ... the former unlicensed bare-knuckle champion, Mr Norman Buckland!' Fackin' hell, I thought to myself, I'd better get back in there sharpish, and promptly left the geezer talking to himself.

As I walked in the room everyone started cheering. I then went straight across and gave Joey Senior and the other faces a handshake and waved in acknowledgment to the rest of the crowd. It was nice to see people cheering; it felt as though these people were holding me in the same high-regard as the other legends that had stood up before me. This was a nice moment for me, knowing I held the prestigious Guv'nor title, but as I've said on so many occasions, the term Guv'nor isn't just about a belt: the title of Guv'nor being bestowed upon a person was a flagging up of their fist-fighting worth across all walks of life. Also, it is a term that is given to many people as an acknowledgement of various other attributes. But in regard to fighting, you will find a Guv'nor in every town, the title the likes of Lenny McLean and Roy Shaw fought for was just an audible title; a title that was gifted to them with the spoken word and not an actual belt to take home and sit in a cabinet. I have always been well-respected for my tasty fists; it was a name that I earned as a very young man! I was first called 'Bruiser' which was a name that my late father Alfie Senior used to call me, something like, "Ere, look at that fackin' Bruiser ... I bet he can have a row ... or ... I bet he can march-on!' Meaning I bet he is a bit of a hard nut. And an accolade of this merit would be bestowed on a person for their graft on the cobbles, as well as in a boxing ring.

So, for me to follow in the footsteps of these fist-fighting legends, was a great honour and no fucking way was I, or am I, ever going to renounce it. I'd fight anyone, anytime, anywhere, and I don't just mean for some soppy belt from someone whose come up from fairyland; some belt that some cunt is always changing the rules with. No ... I mean *any-fackin'-where*. I could be sitting on a toilet and if someone kicked the door in, I would still fight them. I was The Guv'nor, and it was the best feeling in the world. It was also a bonus knowing people as well-respected as Lenny had held the title: I was honoured to have followed in The Guv'nor's footsteps.

I remember an event that had been organised down The Blind Beggar; you know, it was that boozer in East London where that George Cornell geezer had been shot in the head by Ronnie Kray? Well, it was in there, and it was full to capacity with faces from the underworld, oh, and a few fackin' faces from the fantasy underworld showed up as well, probably just to get a look at a few of the real-life naughty fuckers there were plotted about.

Anyway, I was there with my brother and a few other geezers. Alfie was never happy about me fighting on that Mean Machine thing, and him turning up was his way of checking what I was up to. I mean, this wasn't the sort of gaff my brother Alfie would usually be seen at, but Alfie is as sharp as a tack and wanted to let everyone know he was taking me to places they'd never seen, and when Alfie gets a bee in his bonnet about some business venture there ain't no fackin' budging him.

Alfie's idea was to pull me away from the unlicensed fight game! You see, as far as Alfie was concerned, I had won the belt and was the new Guv'nor in town and no one was about to take it away from me. Look, as I've said previously, when I jumped in the ring on the Mean Machine gig I was in my fifties and well past my best. But this was a challenge I just couldn't shy away from, and at the time, I would've fought myself into a fackin' wheelchair to gain the respect that came with the Guv'nor belt thing. But Alfie saw better things for me and didn't like the idea of his brother stepping up into the ring with a fit-as-fuck geezer half his age, fighting to the death, and let's face it, he had a point. Because, by this time, well, according to this specialist geezer down the hospital, I'd had two heart attacks and a stroke, and Alfie, knowing me better than anyone, knew that I would have carried on fighting even if the outcome could have brought on my demise. So, being the big brother and to tame his British bulldog younger brother, he stepped in and told me that my health and my family's welfare was more important than some title; a title that I'd been gifted long before I fought on any of these shows. Alfie said it was time to hang up my gloves and move on.

The Mean Machine boxing promotion company were all there, and I must say that if Alfie hadn't been there too, these geezers could have mustered up my fighter's ego, and won me round. In turn, I'd have signed on the dotted line and defended my title no matter what. But no, that wasn't to be! Alfie, the voice of reason, had a chat with the boys and politely marked their cards, and this was all on the level and completely amicable. See, I'm a loose cannon, and reason just isn't a part of my personality; I go at everything all guns blazing and never think about the consequences. But this time, I needed him by my side, Nanette was worried and that was the last thing I needed. And that was that – it was done – I had retired! Always The Guv'nor, but I'd stepped down with a sense of pride.

The event went well. There I stood, holding court selling these T-shirts in my usual boisterous verbal tones. There I was shouting me mouth off to anyone who would listen, which was everyone given how loud I am, as I roared and bellowed to a sympathetic crowd – they fackin' loved it. Mind you, I think some of them thought I was about to kick off, but I wasn't, they don't know me you see, they probably thought my growling and hollering was done to muster up some sort of aggravation, but it isn't at all, it's bravado – a bit of role play – play acting that most people love.

Towards the end of the day, I was asked if I would come back to fight on their shows again. I told them I was retired but said I would never retire from being The Guv'nor. Almost immediately, I was informed that there was talk about having me shot, and a good mate of mine rang me and said, 'Norm, these boys made you and you've just kicked them to the kerb!' So, I said, 'That isn't how I see it, son. Oh, and now they've threatened to shoot me, so you can tell the cunts to either get the job done or fuck off and leave me to do my thing!' And he replied, 'Listen Norm, it's all bravado … they'll do nothing!' To which I replied, 'Well why not? Because for me, if you say you're going to shoot someone, fackin' get on and do it.' Anyway, it all seemed to blow up to a whole load of fuck all; the threats stopped, and everything went back to normal.

But eh, I'm still The Guv'nor and no number of threats will ever take that away.

As I have mentioned previously, I was also down to fight Dave Courtney, but it didn't come off. Mind you, it was splashed all over the papers, and because someone had thrown Charlie Bronson's name into the pot, the tabloids stated that I was the man who tamed the long-term prisoner. But it was all a load of shit: I've never even met the man. Okay, we were in Woodhill at the same time, but Charlie couldn't mix with any fucker, so how I managed to tame him through a twelve-inch prison door is anyone's fackin' guess. This was all just to sell the story, which in turn would sell their fackin' papers. It was all a load of tabloid bullshit. I respect Charlie for the geezer he is and would never lay claim to such recognition.

Soon after, I was invited to Joey Pyle Senior's 60th birthday bash. But, get this, they wanted to charge me £50 for a fackin' ticket to enter. Anyway, I told them bollocks, and asked them why I had to pay. To which they replied: 'Well, Dave Courtney's paying!' So, I said, 'Well I'm not Dave Courtney ... I'm The fackin' Guv'nor!' After all I had done for them! Why the fuck should I be invited to a do like that and have to pay to get in? After all the money I'd brought to their door – cheeky cunts. Anyway, I've never had a beef with Dave: Dave and I are good pals, so much so that he even ended up being best man at my wedding. As you'd imagine Dave did a really good job: he was as funny and as quick-witted as always, and his speech was well received by our wedding party. Dave had everyone laughing as he recalled tales about what the two of us had got up to over the years.

Like I said earlier, they picked me up and dropped me. I would never be a fackin' puppet to their so-called Guv'nor title. I am my own man and not some idiot who can have his strings pulled. But they didn't listen, and very quickly arranged a new fighter, Decca Heggie, for me to fight. I mean were they taking the fackin' piss or what? It was me and my brother who started this Decca geezer off in the first place; it was me who trained him, me who afforded him all my tips and tricks of the trade, and now these geezers want him to fight me … fackin' hell, I was old enough to be his dad!

To be honest, Decca was alright, but he had obviously become their new puppet and was singing to their tune. And, as I was retired from boxing with the gloves on, I was prepared to stand aside for Decca Heggie and some Welsh geezer to fight it out; I even helped promote it on my Facebook page saying: 'Long live the new Guv'nor,' or something like that. Having said that, due to various reasons, the fight between those two never came off and another fight was set up between ex-professional Julius Francis and Decca. However, due to it being a complete farce I just wasn't prepared to hand my title over to Decca. So, in my eyes I still held the Guv'nor belt and the title that came with it.

This whole Guv'nor belt affair had turned into a fackin' shambles: he said this … she said that … It was all getting a bit boss-eyed, and something was about to kick off. Social media was erupting with all the usual suspects. However, what many didn't know, was that in the past I'd offered every single one of them on there with the biggest mouths the chance to come down to my barn and settle whatever dispute they had with me, but there were no takers. It was fackin' mayhem and to be truthful, it was really starting to give me the hump.

At around this time, I had handed the Stormin' Norman 'Bare-Fist' title belt to a geezer from up north called Gary

Firby. Gary is one of the good ones and a fantastic fighter too. But, as is always the case, the people on social media began 'unintentionally' stoking a fire. You see, because I was known as The Guv'nor everybody on these social media pages started calling the belt I'd handed to Gary 'the Guv'nor belt' but it wasn't, it was the 'Stormin' Norman belt': a belt dedicated to bare-knuckle fighting. My Guv'nor belt was, and still is, tucked away at home, and Alfie has my Roy Shaw Guv'nor belt at his place.

You see, this is where the confusion started because the other camp (mentioned previously) got to thinking I had handed the boxer Gary Firby the Guv'nor title, but I hadn't, this was a different belt altogether. I had had a new belt made and called it the Stormin' Norman Buckland belt, but due to the fact that I was still known as The Guv'nor, everybody believed it to be the Mean Machine Guv'nor's title belt. Anyway, I hope I have managed to clear up the confusion.

People always compare me to the likes of Cliff Fields, Lenny McLean, Roy Shaw, etc. And to me it's a bit disrespectful, 'cos if you asked any one of us the same question, we would all say exactly the same thing, and we certainly wouldn't want to be played against one another. Look, when we were all in our prime and when we were all fit, we feared no one and would fight and beat anyone on the right day. And the reason for this is that each and every one of us, on our best day, was unbeatable: any one of us would have fought King Kong, a Tyrannosaurus Rex, or the fackin' world, it didn't matter. We'd back down from nothing and nobody.

So, to ask me how I would have fared against Shawry, McLean or any of those other geezers just ain't on! Moreover, why don't people ever ask how I'd do against people like West London's Ray Hill, or Hartlepool's Brian Cockerill, or even

Johnny Waldron? Why are people only interested in two fackin' names from that era – it's fackin' relentless. Listen, in my eyes all of those geezers were legends in their own right, and I have far too much respect to play such games. Idiots on those social media pages just love to talk it up and pit fighter against fighter in the hope of rustling up a dead-end debate, and in my eyes they're all a bunch of trouble causers. And to them I say: leave the boys of yesteryear alone with their hard-earned legacies and have a little respect. Furthermore, I guarantee that not one of you mugs would have the balls to run your mouth off at any of us in person.

Which brings me to another point...

In my world we run our lives along a strict code: ya know, like a code of honour. Like back in the days of the Old School gangsters like Joey Pyle Senior, Charlie Richardson, and my great friend (The Godfather of British Crime) Freddie Foreman. Fred and Joe and those boys went by a strict set of rules; ya know, you scratch my back … and all that fackin' stuff. These geezers wouldn't do each other down or say bad things about someone else from their world, and that's the way I have always held myself. If I've got the hump with someone I'll knock on their door, or meet up, and have it out there and then. There's no need for all the fackin' back-stabbing that goes on these days; this new brigade who have seemingly succeeded their ancestors seem to have their wires crossed. And I bet if their fathers were still about, they'd steer them right, or perhaps failing that, give them a belt round the ear'ole for talking out of turn.

You see, at the beginning of all this I was given the biggest gee of all, when they paraded me around like I was some sort of fackin' hero. But it turned out all of that was just to put arses on seats at certain events, and in turn, line the greedy pockets of a certain group of geezers. Because, as soon as I chose to go it alone, these fuckers got the hump and started running their mouths off around town.

'Ere … I even had threats to my life down the blower. Course, this wasn't straight from the man himself. This was executed by a faceless nobody who had obviously been paid a few quid to 'bravely' whisper it down a telephone cable. And as I said to that low-life cunt: 'Don't fackin' say it … do it! Listen, your people know exactly where I rest my head, so get your arse down my gaff and shoot it off on my doorstep! I'm a big enough and ugly enough target, ain't I?'

So, were there any takers? No, of course there fackin' wasn't! These people have too much rabbit, with not enough arse'ole to back it up. But listen, if you think you've got what it takes to put a relatively old geezer out the frame, as I said earlier, please have the courage of your convictions and get your arses down my barn and we'll have a nice little chat.

On the flipside to all that, I really don't want to fall out with anyone; I have respect for the old guard, and in my book, in some small way that passes down to their children and gives them a bit of a get-out-of-jail-free card. So, let's put it to bed here and now – listen to the words you've read. 'Cos let's have it right, no one wants it to get ugly, and nobody more than me wants to go back to the way it was before all of this playground shit.

Why any supposedly respected boxing promoter would bring into dispute his own company over a one-upmanship verbal battle with one of its past prize-fighters is beyond any reasonable intelligence. For what reason would you fuel many haters' argument artillery with actual truth about the way you run your boxing business? Why would you share, in print, the fact that your company is run by charlatans; the fact that your company pays people to take dives simply to feather your own, soon-to-be-barren, nest.

This my friends is beyond any reasonable explanation, not to mention an act that said CEO's forefathers would find questionable and unforgivable. For the simple fact that the code of honour amongst 'the chaps' should undoubtedly trump a person winning some futile argument with one of its own Guv'nors.

But hey, it's done, and unfortunately, once it is in print, not a soul can erase the prose of a lunatic; the detail of which forever remains part of the documentation that holds the entire world of unlicensed boxing accountable of villainy.

Oh well, as Our 'Enry once said:

'It's a funny ol' game!'

17

STORMIN' ONTO THE TELLY BOX

Writers' Note

He took centre stage on the cobbles. He took centre stage on the door. But now it was time for his telly-box light to shine, and boy did he do it his way.

After I became The Guv'nor, the film work started coming in; this suited me down to the ground – I fackin' loved it. Over the years I did a lot of work in front of the camera, loads of stuff came in and everything was going well. The only problem I had was my dyslexia; not being able to read too clever became a bit of a stumbling block when it came to learning my lines. You see, I forgot them all the time, and kept fackin' changing them. I must have drove the crew fackin' bonkers. Mind you, they never said anything, they just kept the camera rolling until I smashed it. Unfortunately, as is always the way with me, the opportunities came flooding in, but my lack of education put the block on most of them. I would've loved to have hit the big-time, and I'm sure that if I'd had the right nurturing, I could've shone, and maybe shot to the stars. Anyway, there's no point crying over spilt milk, so I'll tell you a little about the acting work I did manage to do...

So, Norman 'Brando' (eh, I like the sound of that) stepped up to tread the boards; well, I know I didn't exactly tread the boards, but I didn't know what else to fackin' say, so you'll just have to lump it. Anyway, I had a crack at the old film lark. It was nothing to write home about. Look, I ain't no Oliver Reed, but as you'll have realised by this point in the story, I'll have a go at anything, and when I put my mind to something, most of the time it turns out okay. Let's face it, as an actor I've done more shit than good stuff, but I gave it a good shot and got my name up in lights – well almost. During this little jump in front of the camera, my claim to fame was acting alongside Alex Reid in a film called *Killer Bitch*. Eh, he's a star, isn't he? Well, he is to me. But aside from that, he's a good man all-round, and the director geezer told us that we worked well together.

Anyway, like I said, to date, the films I've done aren't really worth talking about, but it was all a bit of a profile raiser, and it got my name about. And when, like me, you hope to have a book out one day, I imagine that's what it's all about; you do all of this guff in the hope of becoming a bit of a household name.

One day I was on set filming a scene with Alex. Believe it or not, this scene was actually filmed down my barn. Which was great for me, 'cos it was right on my doorstep, literally. Oh, and my kids loved seeing the film world lot round our house, it was something for them to brag about at school. Right, back to the lights, cameras, action...

For the scene we were filming, I had to go at Alex a bit strong. Only thing was, I wasn't used to the film-maker's approach to brawling, and it's completely different going into a tear-up when there's loads of cameras rolling right in front of your face. For some reason I felt like I was about to get nicked! Then my paranoia kicked in, and I started to picture The Sweeney (Sweeney Todd – Flying Squad) running in and shouting: 'YOU'RE NICKED!' There was me thinking to myself, I ain't going to prison for attempted murder in my own backyard for no fucker.

During one part of filming, I let Alex smash into my belly a bit, and make no mistake this boy can hit, and he put some good shots into me for the viewers' pleasure. But, as always, I soaked them up like a pro and stuck my nut into him just to show him who was boss. Then it was my turn to do a bit of choreographed bashing up, and I did, all bravado and hamming it up. Then, after smashing Alex to the floor, I immediately ran at the crowd and hollered at them: 'Right, who's fackin' next?' Unbeknown to me at the time (something I spotted on the monitor thing later) there was this young-un at the back and he looked terrified; he looked like he was about to have fackin' kittens, the poor little fucker! I was only playing up to the cameras. Having said that, the petrified lad had a big American Pitbull with him, and I bet that wouldn't have said no to a fackin' tear-up.

As I'm sure you all know, Alex was also a pretty good martial arts fighter, and he'd had a few of those fights that they do in them cage things. Anyway, in one part of a scene I smashed a few shots into him, I obviously made sure I didn't go in too strong, but I must've got carried away a bit and grabbed him by the bollocks, and to be brutally honest, he did squeal a bit. With that, the director Liam Galvin came over and told me to lighten up a bit. So I did as I was told, and it went very well, and Alex and I had a right fackin' laugh while doing it.

Now, to make it look more real I said to Alex, 'Kick me as hard as you can,' and fuck me he didn't hold back, as he almost took me off my fackin' pins! What you got to remember is that he was trained in this; he did really well in the game and over the years he had put a few 'faces' away inside that cage. Anyway, it did the trick, and we ended up having a right old half choreographed tear-up. Oh, but we had to do about twenty different takes, 'cos I kept changing my fackin' lines again. There was Alex doing all his famous kicks and kneeings, then I just screamed at him to smash me in the stomach as hard as he could with some combinations. This he did, and the two of us ended up in the spit, sand and stone on the floor. Then after putting him away 'for the camera' I was just about to smash a breeze block over his face when, as directed, I was shot in the head before I had the chance to do it.

There I stood, pumping with adrenaline, with a ton of sweat dripping off me. I was all made up with a bullet wound that was oozing blood (which the director kept squeezing out of a bottle onto the cut) out of me, which was running down into my eye. And all the time I'm stood there screaming, holding this breeze block above my head. Well, after a few takes of me dropping it onto my own head, we finally nailed it. But fuck me, it was a lot of hard work, and to be honest, I didn't know the film game could be that difficult.

He's a tough old boy is Alex. The geezer is a lovely man, full of passion, yet for some reason, for the most part he's a little misunderstood. Mind you that bird he was hooked up with off the telly didn't do him any favours; he should've binned her off the first night he met her. I ribbed him a bit about that on set, but it was all in good fun and all just for the cameras. Liam Galvin and his missus Yvette Rowland always took good care of me, and it was nice to play-fight for a change rather than do it for real.

During one scene we had to wrap this man up in barbed-wire, and in another scene I was filmed holding a shotgun to a geezer's head. We also filmed a scene in a pub over in Aylesbury, where the film-makers had all the locals jump me. This was hard to do, but I had to make it look real. The strange thing was, after all this macho shit, a few weeks later it was reported in the tabloids that Alex Reid was a cross-dresser; I don't know if it was a publicity stunt or if he just got his kicks from dressing in women's clothes. But anyway, who gives a fuck if Alex smashes on a bird's dress and it makes him feel alive? Who are we to fackin' judge? It's nobody's business but his own. Although, the papers did try their best to make a cunt of him, but I bet the gutless fuckers wouldn't take the piss if he reared up on them.

In April 2010, I attended the UK premiere party (for the film above, *Killer Bitch*) at the Curzon Mayfair in London. It was a fantastic night and we got to chat about the laughs we'd had while filming. The likes of Roy Shaw, Dave Courtney and the boxer Robin Reid were all in attendance, as was the lovely Yvette Rowland who played the leading lady. But for some reason, the star of the film, Alex Reid, was a no-show; I'm sure he had his reasons. Obviously, the paparazzi were there in waiting outside the barriers of the red carpet. And I gave them a right show as I turned up in full bloom in an immaculate white suit, a brown fur coat, dripping in all my Tom and finery. I obviously stopped to pose for the photos, as it was obvious they wanted me to do some theatricals. So, not wanting to disappoint them, I gave them a load of, 'Who's the Fackin' Guv'nor?' chants, as I made my way to do various interviews.

A little while later, I was up in London for Dave Courtney's 60th birthday party; I think it was the following year. This time, Alex Reid was there, so I wasted no time in winding him up and ripping the arse out of him while he laughed and hollered: 'Fuck this, I'm off!' and walked off, pretending to have the hump, while he was laughing at me. He's a good man Alex, he can take a joke and doesn't mind you taking the piss. I did look for him a little later in the evening, but unfortunately he had left. Hopefully, I'll catch up with him at my major concern, book signing.

In 2014 I played a bit part of a hooligan in a film by Michael Lindley and Nick Nevern called *The Hooligan Factory*. At that time, that Nick geezer was getting his head in everywhere: he played the lead role of Dex in this film that we were in but was mainly known for the *Essex Boys* films and *The Sweeney* film with Ray Winstone from a couple of years earlier. I only played a hooligan, but my boys got their faces on film too, so that was a real bonus.

I also did a part for Channel 4's *Big Brother* where they had me on the screen, all loud and boisterous, selling off the entire props from past shows. I was like Del Boy (from the TV series *Only Fools and Horses*) with the hump as I screamed at the screen, urging the public to buy Vinnie Jones's underpants and Alex Reid's fake tan. They even had a song similar to 'Hooky Street' playing in the background. There was one bit where I said: 'If you don't like standing up, well get this sofa then as used by proper celebrities ... oh, and by Dane Bowers as well!' Sorry Dane ... I didn't write it. My name for this captivating bit of Fly-Pitching TV was 'Small 'Arry', and at the end, some bird narrated over it, saying: 'Nought per cent finance and free credit with every purchase ... you lucky slags! But, if you don't keep up the payments, Small 'Arry will come round and kick you in the Davinas!' (Davina McCall's – Balls)

In 2016 I landed another part in a low-budget film called *Gatwick Gangsters*. And would you believe it, guess what part I was offered? Yeah, you got it: I was to play a gangster called Goldie and ended up getting the shit kicked out of me by this actor geezer. But again, I had to work out how to make it look like I was being beaten. The film had a big cast that included the darts player Bobby George, the late snooker player Willie Thorne, and Garry Bushell and Dave Courtney had roles in it, too! Okay, the film was a bit iffy, but it was all good experience.

Me and my boxer pal Matt Legg did a film called *New City Fighter*; this one wasn't too bad for a small budget film, as it was filmed by a promising up-and-coming film-maker called Russell North. Apparently, the film that was based on Matt's life was only supposed to have run for about ten minutes, and it was all to do with prison and boxing and the dirty life that you can get yourself mixed up in. But as it turned out, the film ended up running for an hour. Being such a low-budget film made it that little bit more special and because we didn't have access to hospitals, prisons, clubs and bars, etc, everything had to be thought out and scrutinised ten-fold, in line with the lack of dough in the company's coffers.

Fortunately, they ended up producing a great little film, and it still has a cult following to this day. The story was sort of true to life, which went along the lines of Matt going to prison, meeting me, and me training him up for greatness with a shot at a boxing title. So, what was actually printed to film was simply us re-enacting our prison days. We were filming the boxing scene from jail one day and I said to Matt, 'Matt, make it look a bit real ... give me a belt on the nose so that you draw blood!' With that, Matt smashed me with a cruncher of a shot, and he's only gone and broken my fackin' 'ooter! There was blood pouring out all over the gaff, but I didn't give a fuck, as it was just everyday run-of-the-mill life for me and Matt. It was a good experience for us both, and in my case, it was invaluable: it helped me get a handle on the film game, as I was given a lot of dialogue to get my teeth into.

I also did a little tour on the stage talking about my life. This one night we did a show at the MK Stadium, and our 'An Audience With …' style show was called 'Norman and his Firm Friends' and it went down a storm. It was fantastic, and very busy, with hundreds of people in attendance. The strange thing was, they'd added my adopted godfather Ray Carter to the poster board as 'Uncle 'Arry', a name that has stuck to this day; having said that I think Uncle 'Arry actually prefers it to his real name. Anyway, it was a fantastic night, filled with stories, laughs and giggles, and, because it was my birthday, an added surprise of a birthday cake was handed to me.

As a special guest we had the great Brummy boxer Errol 'Bomber' Graham. Errol was a true boxing great and a gentleman. Our film man Russell North and all the staff at the venue helped out and made it a great success. The night was dedicated to raising money for the local bowel cancer unit at the Milton Keynes Hospital, and with the help of a fantastic raffle and quality auction pieces from Signature Auctions, we were able to hand over a considerable bundle of dough. So, everyone involved was over the moon.

In 2019, Manny got me a bit of work on a film called *Little Bastards*, which was a low budget Brit flick about gangsters in South London. This was another bit of good experience, and I made a few friends and contacts while filming. One day during filming, we were all in this room with a load of guns and I had to drag some geezer over a table. Anyway, just as I was in the middle of it, Manny jumped up and hollered, 'Fackin' hell, you don't have to act do you Norm? You're just playing yourself, doing what you do on an average fackin' day!' He can be a funny facker can old Manny – he's a good man as well.

More recently, a mate of mine called me up and said they were looking for interesting people and stories for the ITV programme *Judge Rinder*. He said they thought I would be good for it as I was a bit of a character. Me and my Nanette had a bit of a laugh with the Judge and his crew, and I managed to get my face recognised up and down the country a little bit more.

The Judge and I exchanged a right bit of banter between us, with him telling me he had a black belt in fackin' Judo, and me telling him that in the house of law he was every inch The Guv'nor, which was great for the viewers.

Judge Rinder asked me what it meant to be The Guv'nor, ya know, of the unlicensed boxing game. So I told him, and we had a laugh and a joke about him being The Guv'nor and I said that I wouldn't fight him 'cos he was the boss in the courtroom. It was all in good humour, and I think I managed to present myself in a slightly different light. The people got to see another side of me, as opposed to the boisterous growling lunatic that is often talked about.

During the programme I managed to set a few records straight that had been playing on my mind. I managed to explain the reasons why I could no longer fight on the unlicensed circuit anymore yet was able to highlight my passion for the Guv'nor and its belt was still at the top of my list, and that I'd handed it over to a worthy fighter called Gary Firby. I also mentioned that I was done with the game and that Gary could pick up the mantle where I left off. This all came across extremely well, and everyone that watched it said that even without all my usual snarling, growling and bravado I still managed to show my charismatic side. So, hopefully, this and the rest of the stuff I've done on the telly box will lead to more TV work in the not-too-distant future.

I ended up doing a lot of filming with the YouTube noteworthy Liam Galvin, who had filmed that *Killer Bitch* film I mentioned earlier. Whenever there was a boxing show at Caesars, Liam would be there, and over the years I have done quite a few interviews with the man and his crew. We filmed one interview over at Dave Courtney's house, Camelot Castle. In this little bit of VT (videotape), Liam and his team interviewed me and another notable gangland figure called Charlie Breaker. As usual, Dave was on top form, and as I'm sure a lot of you know, with Dave, what you see is what you get: he's a colourful character who, under the right management, would've taken America by storm. I believe the Yanks would have taken to his chippy dialogue and ready wit, as they love all of that British celebrity gangster stuff across the pond. And, let's face it, they don't come more street-style gangster celeb than the good old Yellow Pages of British crime.

We also did a charity event to raise money for a young boy who had had a terrible accident over in Maryport. The headline in the *Times and Star* read: Adrian Kirkbride (Kirky) of Brick-Top Productions is bringing five well-known boxers down to tell the young children some stories about the ups and downs of their lives. Apparently, what had happened was, this geezer Kirky's son, Odin, fell from a ten-foot rugby stand, and landed headfirst onto the concrete, which smashed in his skull. According to the papers, the poor little fella had had two bleeds on his brain and as a result spent a couple of months in Alder Hey Children's Hospital in Liverpool. Throughout this little boy's ordeal, he had to have loads of time off school, and apparently, the school and the kids had supported him so well through it that Kirky wanted to thank them, and staging the event and pulling in some much-needed cash was his way of doing it. At the event was me, my brother Alfie, Matt Legg, and good old Ray 'Uncle 'Arry' Carter, who was the late Roy Shaw's driver. And if you want somebody to tell stories of the good, the bad and the ugly in life, Uncle 'Arry is your man.

18

THE GUV'NOR HAS LEFT THE BUILDING

Writers' Note
Life throws up all kinds of obstacles, and for Norman, that reality was no different, perhaps even a little more taxing. However, he took them on, took them in, and gave them a place in his heart, unaware that it was there where his strife would begin.

Looking back over the years, it's clear to see I was a right fackin' handful! I've bitten people's ears and noses off in tear-ups; I've stamped on geezers, and I've even pulled a twelve-bore out to use as a frightener. I've done the fackin' lot. But I had to: otherwise, these nasty cunts would've bitten off my bits and pieces instead.

I've always used my nut in a row, and I don't mean in a 'using me noddle' sort of sense, no, I mean I've used it as a battle-tool. And with the size of my nut, the effects were often devastating. But look, it was the only life I knew, and I had to win at any cost. I mean, these days I've obviously slowed down a bit. Although this is born out of necessity, as I have my wife and kids to look after and getting myself in all kinds of trouble and getting sent down for another serving of porridge, really isn't where I wanna be these days.

To be brutally honest, I have actually mellowed a lot with age. However, that's probably down to the fackin' heart problems: the choice was simply taken away from me. But back when I was in the thick of it, back in the days when the mantra was anything goes, during a time when it wasn't a guarantee that the Old Bill would come knocking, I would have bitten someone's bollocks off to get a result in a row. But listen, they would have done the same to me, mark my words, that was a twenty-four-carat certainty.

The thing is, when you come unstuck and get wound up, the beast and its killer instinct steps in. I don't know why I had the cunt inside me, or where it came from. I don't know if I was paying a penance for something I'd done in a previous life, but, no matter what the history, it was a part of me, stubborn, unrelenting, glued to me, and there was fuck-all I could do about it. Perhaps it was woven into my fackin' Levis (genes); perhaps it was filtered down through the family DNA, fused into my blood from my great-great-grandfather, George Cooper. Nevertheless, for me it will remain a mystery, for this Jekyll and Hyde that I've long since cast aside was always there, it was like a bad penny that cropped up just when it fackin' felt like it.

But like I've said, these days I've opted for a quiet life. Now, don't get me wrong, the gloves are still there; still hung up down the barn in case I need to fire myself up again. But eh, nowadays they're a bit more of an ornament, a trophy of days gone by, and I won't stick them on my hands until someone really upsets me. If someone harms my family, my kids, the pets, or, God forbid, my beautiful rock through life Nanette, then, and only then, will they be pulled from the wall and I'll quickly spring into action – just like the old days.

Look, I'm fifty-eight and I've had two or three attacks to my heart, plus a stroke. I've been shot, stabbed, gassed to fuck, and I'm still here breathing, still The fackin' Guv'nor, and nothing or no one will ever take that away from me. I'll still help people who are in need; I'll still rush to the aid of friends who are down on their luck and need a helping hand, always and forever, just like the song says. Now, who is that record by? I fackin' love that record, anyway, shut up Norm you're distracting yourself. Right, where was I? Oh yeah, I was telling you how fackin' lavvly I am! But as I said, it doesn't take much to muster-up the lunatic, just like the other day when I was working down the uncovered market.

... *'Ere, get on this...*

It was a Sunday morning. I was down the market watching over the stallholders and punters, and making sure no one was being manipulated or bullied, when I heard a commotion over by the main gate, so I shot over to investigate. Apparently, the fracas centred around a certain foreign contingent who weren't happy to be parting with a few bits of paper with the Queen's face on, who didn't want to pay like the rest of the customers – fackin' selfish gits. So I said, 'Just toe the line fellas and pay your dues like the rest of us!' But no, these fuckers are obviously entitled and thought they were a better class of person to every fucker else! Well, not on The Guv's watch. 'Listen,' I went on. 'You're paying, or you can fuck off down the road!'

At this point I was still being nice, and said, 'Listen boys ... c'mon ... we don't want this to get out of hand ... so pay the good lady, and we can get on with our business and enjoy this lavvly sunny day.' Suddenly, the littlest one of the bunch flared up, and went right in on the lady owner and spat right in her fackin' face! Well, that's done it, the gloves are off:

these boys needed a bit of a spanking, so I've given it to them all! The growling stopped and I was taking the cunts apart as a group – it was mayhem, and there were bodies all over the shop.

Immediately, they've seen a bit of sense, picked themselves up and had it away. Mind you, obviously feeling a bit embarrassed, they've decided to get on the blower (phone) and call-up the cavalry for a bit of back-up. Horrible bastards, they think they've been hard done to, and it's them who've spat in a lady's face. Spat in her face 'cos she was enforcing the rules of the market? Well, they can fuck right off, and if they wanna get dirty, I can get a lot fackin' dirtier. Fortunately for them, the Old Bill turned up, and everything got sorted at the hands of the law. You see, it never stops: there is trouble around every corner. Mind you, stuff like this isn't solely reserved for our country, because out there in other far-off lands there are horrible cunts lurking around every corner as well.

When we were in the Philippines, Nanette and I were out having a nice relaxing walk, taking in the beautifully picturesque scenery when we stumbled upon a family, and when I say stumbled, I mean almost literally, because this poor unfortunate family of locals were huddled up at the roadside together, with nowhere to go, and no place to call home. They even had a little baby in a box on a bike trailer, sleeping; the poor little thing was covered in bites from flying insects. It broke our hearts. Fackin' hell, I remember thinking to myself, how often we take life for granted. I mean, at times I think my life is hard, but when you imagine what this homeless family were going through, it makes you reassess your own selfish brainbox. I just wanted to bundle them up and take them back home to a nice warm and loving family.

While chatting with them for a while I asked (as it was Christmastime) what they were doing to celebrate, and a big fat nothing came back in response. I was gutted for them, and I thought this can't be right! So, while I'm tucking into the finest festive grub, with all the regalia of a fine Christmas lunch, these poor fuckers will be here, sat in the same place, with nothing but each other and a whole load of memories. Well, I thought, not on The Guv'nor's watch, this definitely isn't happening. So, I went off to a local shop and bought them more cakes, treats and grub than they'd probably seen in years. Then, I said to them, if they were there on Christmas Day, I would come back for them, and they could celebrate Christmas with me and my family.

The father looked as though he was about to break down. So, I said, 'No need for all that, for the next few days you're all a part of my family; we'll have a party fit for a king ... something you will remember for a lifetime.' Unfortunately, it wasn't to be, because when I went back, they were gone. I was told they'd been hit by a gang of 'Snatchers' from the area (Snatchers are horrible, unruly kids who will nick anything from you to sell; they'd even take the baby's rattle if it brought enough dough in to buy a bag of meth.) It was a shame, but at least they ate well for a few days, I can rest easy thinking about that.

Oh, wait a second, did I tell you about the first holiday I went on that led to me meeting my wife? Mind you, at the time she didn't realise it was her destiny...

So, let's just call her 'my future wife' for this bit. Knowing how my life could be, I didn't want to take her back with me and put her through hell, so I went searching for a fortune teller in a village near the town to set the record straight. We found the directions and after a bit of a drive arrived at the geezer's house.

We knocked on the door and entered. Now, because of my gran and my Romany roots I have always been a big believer in all spiritual stuff, but my idea was to let Nanette know exactly what she was letting herself in for. This way I wouldn't have a chance to ruin her future if the reading flagged-up something bad. I loved her and wanted the very best for her. So, the geezer did a reading with the cards and said he could see I would be honest and true to her but asked her to come back on her own at a later date for another reading.

Apparently, at the next reading he informed her that I would love her forever and that no one else could love her except me. He also mentioned that I suffered with stress and anxiety and needed to be in good company to relax; he basically told her everything ... warts 'n' all. He told Nanette that things would be very difficult at times, but she'd have to be patient with me, and in time everything would be fantastic. Another thing he was bang on about was, he said we would get married and live together, which was also true 'cos we have been together through thick and thin ever since. Nanette is an amazing, patient and resourceful woman – I couldn't live without her – I love her to pieces.

Before I became aware of the heart attacks and stroke I'd had, I used to think I was bulletproof, and after surviving all of that, I would probably believe it even more. However, a couple of years ago, I went to work and received what must've been a bit of a warning. In fact, a specialist told me recently that back in 2018 I must have suffered a minor stroke. This was obvious to him, but I didn't realise it at the time.

What happened was, my nose started running and my lips went all strange: they were moving independently, and I couldn't get my words out properly. At the time, I thought this was just me being me, as many crazy things have happened to me over the years, and this little oddity was nothing new. Oh, and I couldn't feel my ear, and my arms started to twitch! Suddenly, my legs started going a bit wobbly, but instead of sitting down like any normal person, I decided to dance it off: I was like Michael Jackson doing his *Thriller* bit, only far better looking. Anyway, I got in my car and took myself off to work. While driving along it was running round my mind as I tried to work out what the fuck was wrong with me. Once I got to work everything seemed okay, but whenever I took a sip out of a cup of tea, there was no taste at all – it was extremely weird. So, it was straight back to bed with my angel Nanette by my side; Nanette was a lot more worried than she was letting on, and afterwards told me that even my kids were worried too. Apparently, the kids said, if Dad's frightened, it must be something bad.

My boss at that time had brought himself an ex-police dog, an Alsatian, for security on site, and I was down there doing a bit of graft, moving a load of heavy metal frames to build into a cage. Anyway, because I hadn't been sleeping for a few nights, Nanette had been in touch with my doctor and given him the SP on my situation. This all seemed like a load of shit for nothing to me. Anyway, a bit later the doc phoned Nanette back and asked her to take my pulse. This she immediately did, and informed the doctor that it was firing like a tommy gun; she said it was like one long line with no pauses. Fuck me, I thought to myself, 'That means I'm dead, doesn't it?' I must say I did feel rough as fuck, and I even thought it might be a heart attack. With that, they immediately sent an ambulance and got me to the hospital a bit lively. Obviously I didn't want to go, and I told Nanette to tell them that I was good as gold, but deep down I knew something was badly wrong. I think my heart was fighting for its fackin' life: being attacked and abused for so many years I think it had finally had enough.

When I arrived at the hospital, they put me straight into a bed, and minutes later my wife Nanette arrived. Knowing how scared I was and how panicked Nanette was, the hospital sorted out a room for her, it was only up the road a couple of blocks away, and my beautiful Nanette never left my side for one second.

While I was in hospital my lung gave up, I had an infection in my liver, and was having terrible trouble breathing. At one stage my wife put her hand on my head thinking I was dead, and instantly ran from the room and went in search of a nurse. Immediately, the nurse informed her that I was okay, but that I was fighting for my life. And all this while I was just lying there thinking, I've never been much of a drinker, I've never smoked as much as one single cigarette, let alone anything fackin' stronger, and yet here I am lying in a hospital bed playing Russian Roulette with the fackin' Devil. Had I been so bad in life, and this was my payback, I wondered?

Now, some of you may laugh at me for this, but what I want to do when I die is explore the universe. I mean, I don't know how I'm going to put this into action, I'll probably have to have a word with Him upstairs so that He can make it happen. You see, due to my Romany upbringing I've always been a big believer in the hereafter. When I was ill in hospital for ten weeks, in my coma, I had all sorts of dreams, and one of them really sticks in my mind because of how real it felt. This was a dream I had about a big fackin' spaceship; this big machine was flitting through the universe like a bat out of hell and I was fighting all these aliens, trying to get hold of them.

My Nanette said that sometimes she would see me reaching my hands out in front of me as if I was trying to grab hold of something. And like a lot of dreams when you're poorly, everything seems so real, and to me it felt like I was living it out in real time. Now, I'm not sure if it was the medication I was on, or if I actually did trip off on a journey to the stars, but whatever it was I was going through, I remember thinking to myself, 'Where the fuck are my wife and kids? I should be with them … not flying off around the fackin' galaxy on my own!' I was trying my hardest to escape this dark, unknown place, when suddenly, the next thing I knew, I was awake and completely out of the coma. What a fackin' trip!

Once out of the coma I was released from hospital and was at home trying my best to get back to everyday life and some sort of normality. I bought some canaries (like the ones I looked after when I was in the nick) for my stress, because the specialist had said that things such as this were supposed to be good for the heart. After a few days had passed, I kept asking my wife and friends where the green canary had gone. I kept on and on about it for about four days and started to think that Nanette and my pals were just being fackin' stubborn not giving me any answers. But it turned out I never even had a green one; turns out it was all in my head. And it wasn't until a short time later, we realised it must have been the medication. Anyway, I was driving my missus and friends crazy.

Like I say, I'm now living a more tranquil life, well, I don't know how true that is, because at times my life is anything but! For one thing, my kids are fackin' nuts! The boys aren't really a problem anymore, but my beautiful yet slightly cranky daughter Siobhan (named after my mum) can be a loose fackin' cannon. She's just like me: she's wired up slightly wrong and turns into a raving lunatic. She's a beautiful pretty young thing, but when she loses it, she just doesn't give a fuck for nobody.

A little while back she got into some dispute with the manager of the local McDonald's fast-food place and lost her head and put one of the gaff's big fackin' windows in; cost a fortune those things, and you can guarantee old muggins here was going to have to foot the bill. According to Siobhan and her pal who was with her at the time, this manager was being a bit cocky with her friend, and Siobhan hating a bully, lost it and went nuts! (Well, that's my girl, the apple doesn't fall too far from the tree.) Anyway, that was that, and I had to take a trip down the Old Bill shop to sort it out.

Look, I ain't into her kicking off and putting windows in, according to a few bystanders this manager geezer had manhandled her a bit! I mean come on, she was only fourteen years old, she's a little dainty girl for fuck's sake. Well anyway, I wasn't happy about that and told them exactly how I felt when I arrived, saying: 'Look, she's got a bit riled up and done something that she shouldn't, but your man (the manager geezer) put his hands on her and got a bit heavy.' Listen, I was overdramatising a bit, 'cos I didn't want to have to fork out a couple of grand for a fackin' window. Look, my girl must be going through hormones or something, I don't know what's wrong with her, but eh, she can get a bit fackin' loopy at times. Thankfully, they saw reason, weighed up the odds of me kicking up a fuss about the abuse to my daughter; plus the fact they know me and were probably worried about me taking the matter up with the manager geezer personally. Thankfully, my mild-mannered intimidation worked, and they just gave her a telling-off: a caution. So it was all sorted

– I left it at that. Mind you, here's a word to the gaffer of the McDonald's: next time, watch how you handle my daughter, 'cos the last thing you want is me with the hump paying you a visit.

As I mentioned, my Siobhan is a lot like me, she's tough and doesn't take any prisoners. She also has a heart of gold, which is fantastic, but she brings all sorts of waifs and strays home who are down on their luck, and immediately offers them a place of sanctuary. Now, this is all lovely, but it always ends up costing me fackin' money. Oh, and any young boys out there who set their eye on Siobhan please be aware! Because, as I have said to her most recent boyfriend, 'Whatever you do to my darlin' daughter … I will do to you. So, before you lay your hands on her, I want you to think long and hard about what I've said. And if you hurt her … well I won't have to do fuck all, 'cos sunshine, my girl will have already done it!'

I've mentioned the problems that came from the heart attack, but there have been some positives too. One of those things is my heart health when I get a bit aggie, it's a hell of a lot more stable to what it used to be. You see before the operation, if ever I got irritated my heart would pump like a pneumatic fackin' drill; it would almost pump its way out of my chest, and my breathing would go all wobbly. But ever since the surgery, all of that seems to have become more stable, and these days I hardly ever feel out of breath.

Like this one day while out having a nice relaxing drive with my wife...

One day we were driving along, happily, when I came to a stop at a roundabout. As it was my right of way I eased out, then suddenly a man (who wasn't paying attention to the road) appeared and cut me right up. Well, I immediately saw red and began flashing my lights for him to pull over and have it out. This geezer was also going mad at the wheel, so I hurried on a bit and pulled up at the side of him. Then, when I peered into his motor, I noticed he was in his senior years, and thought right, I'll leave it at that. But then he wound down his fackin' window and spat at me. So now, I just wanted to kill him; I was fackin' furious, I was going off my head and my wife was getting a little worried for the other geezer's life. With that, I calmed myself down and fucked off before I got into some proper road rage; I just didn't need it. You see by this point, my heart would usually have taken ages to go back to its resting beats, but ever since my surgery, within seconds it had gone back to normal. I felt great and went on with my day totally relaxed.

I mentioned that utter wrong-un Jimmy Savile earlier on, and it's weird 'cos that cunt seems to keep causing me agg everywhere I fackin' go…

In 2019, my young boy Alfie was rushed into hospital for an emergency operation, and when we got there, they told us someone had to stay with him. Apparently, this was due to changes in their security because of what that dirty lowlife pervert had been up to years earlier, so someone had to stay through the nights with my Alfie. Turns out he was on the same ward where that pervert carried out his perving. Fackin' hell, I wished he'd have been about when Alfie was in 'cos my boy would've pulled his silly blond hair out and bitten off his nose. Then I'd have ripped his bollocks off for him, the dirty horrible cunt.

Fortunately, Alfie only had to stay in for one night, and my Nanette did the nursing, which was a blessing, 'cos I'd have probably dozed off and someone might have swiped him. Mind you, at the minute that wouldn't be a bad thing, 'cos the little twat is playing up and won't go to school; he keeps running off and no one knows where he is. I said to the school I'd rather him stay at home, at least that way we know where he is. He's a right little chip off the old block, that boy.

But, joking apart, my family are my life! Not in that 'King of the Fackin' Castle' kind of way; not in that 'you touch my kith and kin, and I will kill you' kind of way, obviously that part goes without saying. What I mean is, without these people in my life, my life wouldn't be worth living.

As you've learned by now, I had a hard upbringing, being ridiculed and taunted for the troubled child I was, but I was just a young boy and didn't have the capacity to take it all in. In more recent years, I have reassessed my values and realised that these people that I love to pieces accept me for what I am. I'm loud, boisterous and overbearing! Straight-talking, fiery and unyielding. But I have a loving side, and when love takes over, the beast in my head takes a back seat. And when that horrible fucker is bashed up, beaten and broken, I can relax and get on with my life in the best way I see fit. I've always had a lot of love in my heart, but unfortunately the bullies and horrible nasty people never gave themselves the opportunity to see it. And from the very first day I was mocked and insulted, I reluctantly cast the nice geezer in the bin and the beast inside stepped in.

However, as I keep saying, most of those days are behind me now. Because, in the comfort of my loving family's non-judging safe haven, this loveable lunatic with the heart of a lion will always be a winner. 'I'm The Guv'nor ... and this moniker that I earned while putting my life on offer for others will stay with me forever.'

Oh, just one last thing...

'Who's the Fackin' Guv'nor?'